Rock the Audition

Rock the Audition

How to Prepare for and Get Cast in Rock Musicals

SHERI SANDERS

Hal Leonard Books
An Imprint of Hal Leonard Corporation

Published in 2011 by Hal Leonard Books
An Imprint of Hal Leonard Corporation
7777 West Bluemound Road
Milwaukee, WI 53213

Trade Book Division Editorial Offices
33 Plymouth St., Montclair, NJ 07042

Printed in the United States of America

Book design by Adam Fulrath

Library of Congress Cataloging-in-Publication Data

Sanders, Sheri.
  Rock the audition : how to prepare for and get cast in rock musicals / Sheri Sanders.
      p. cm.
  Includes index.
  ISBN 978-1-4234-9943-5
  1. Musicals–Auditions. I. Title.
  MT956.S35 2011
  783'.066143–dc22
                          2011002123

www.halleonardbooks.com

To Amy Rogers

Contents

Foreword

I met Sheri Sanders in January 2007 when we were rehearsing a benefit for the American Theatre Festival in upstate New York. She sang a song from a new rock musical and I played. There was something special about our rehearsal: it felt refreshing and creative. We discussed tempo, how the grooves progressed, dynamics and emotional tone . . . Sheri was in touch with all the dimensions of the music.

At the end of that rehearsal, I looked at her and said, very honestly and somewhat impulsively, "I like you!"

Sheri: "I like you too!"

Me: "I don't normally want to chat like this with people, but I feel like I could talk with you all day."

Sheri: "Let's be friends."

And from that moment we were. Over the next few days we discussed God, music, our histories, relationships, and dreams. It wasn't the kind of friendship in which one "holds back." This is what having a relationship with Sheri is like.

Soon after, I started playing for Sheri's Rock the Audition classes (I even took a series of classes as a student, which was incredible!). And I discovered that Sheri teaches in the same way she does everything: she shares. She doesn't hoard her experiences, knowledge, or ideas; she gives them to you. When Sheri teaches, she isn't there to show you how smart she is. She is there to help you unlock your personal expression.

I'd like to give you an overview of the Rock the Audition workshop: each session includes four 4-hour classes. During the course of the four weeks, you, the student, work musically and dramatically on two contrasting pop/rock songs. Sheri personally chooses these songs based on your vocal ability and distinct personality. Her work is so personalized that there is no feeling of competition in the room. Instead, there is an air of honesty, excitement, and support.

In rock class I have played for actors who don't really sing, as well as highly skilled pop/rock theater performers. I have played for "legit" singers who have never had the confidence to try this type of music. Sheri finds a path for every single student.

Have you ever had someone shape a song to fit you, instead of molding you to fit their concept of the song? This is what you learn to do in Rock the Audition. One night, a lovely actress was singing "Angels from Montgomery" (as covered by Bonnie Raitt). Sheri wanted to distract her from thinking too much as she sang and asked her to start the song at the piano, and then trace the lines of the floor tiles with her feet. As this singer looked down, pacing and tracing the tiles carefully with her toes, her song became increasingly honest, simple, and vulnerable. She came to a place of stillness and emotional connection that was achingly real. And we got to "see" her, not just hear a cool song.

Another actor was assigned "Rosanna" (recorded by Toto). Sheri suggested that he sing the song like he was doing an '80s video but completely serious and full of *drama*. He hung on a curtain, did *Footloose* dance moves, put up his collar—it was hilarious! And he sang with greater conviction than ever before. He was set free to use the full extent of his own imagination.

You see, Sheri is a door opener, an obstacle remover, a path finder. She clears the way for you to move forward discovering avenues that you haven't yet traveled emotionally, dramatically, physically, and vocally. She is an enabler in the best sense of the word.

This "magic" doesn't end in her studio. In the following pages you will receive the keys that will unlock new personal expression. You will take it and make it personal for you. And chances are you will surprise yourself and the people behind the table at your next audition.

I think that the central message in this book is about relationship. You have a relationship to your song. Lyrically, you connect to the feelings and attitudes you express through the text. You express the music through your body and vocal stylizations. You have a relationship with your pianist, your partner in expressing rhythmic mood, period, emotion, and attitude. You have yet another relationship to the room, to the creative team behind the table, to the outfit you choose . . . are you getting the idea? EVERYTHING is about relationship. That means that you are the co-creator of this musical experience. And you can't be in a bubble. You've got to share yourself.

Congratulations on opening this book. Believe me when I say that these pages are full of practical *and* inspired information. They are full of the heart and spirit of Sheri. So have fun and have faith that you are doing something very good for yourself.

Wendy Bobbitt Cavett
Music Director, *Mamma Mia!*
Broadway
2011

Acknowledgments

This book would never have been possible without the undeniable generosity of my dear mother, Ann, and without the support of my loving father, Don, and his sweetiepie, Ruby. Big thanks to Amy Rogers for seeing me so clearly, and to the amazing students I get to play with at Pace University. Extra special thanks to Robert Meffe for working with me on the historical chapters! Profound thanks to my soul sister Wendy Bobbitt Cavett, and my other music directors: Brad Simmons, Mark Fifer, and Zach Dietz. Worship to my trusty roundtable: Stacia Newcomb, Kristina Teschner, Liz Asti, Lisa Rochelle, Ravi Roth, and my beautiful acting teacher Kimberly Vaughn—thanks for reading my book and giving me feedback on my book AS I WAS WRITING IT! Mike Diehl . . . thanks for running around online for me! Tiffany Quist, Claudia Reinhardt Johnson, and Michael Ferraiuolo at True Voice Studios, YOU ROCK! Big Love and gratitude to David Finkle, Mary-Mitchell Campbell, Celisse Henderson, Betsy Capes, and Jodie Capes at Capes Coaching, Matt Corozine, my manager Kevin Thompson, and my channeler Judith Pomerantz. WT McRae, THANK YOU for creating my logo; you're amazing! Thank you Lisa Clayton for your web design genius, and Dirty Sugar Photography for making me look so damn hot! Who knew!?

The friends who created the DVD for this book deserve highest praise. To Matthew Brookshire, "The Schermerhorn," and The Actors Fund, much appreciation. Gregory McDonald, Ravi Roth, Kymberli McKanna, and Justin Gentry, you are my sweeties. Thank You. Tom Burke. God, thank you. Loving thanks to Kimberly Vaughn. Jac Chairs is the best cinematographer ever. Nathan Manley, you sound designed, edited, and created all of the amazing graphics for my DVD, and I am in shock and awe at your talent. My deepest thanks goes to Stacia Newcomb for not only producing this DVD and being a creative *geeeeenius* but for caring for me and supporting me like a sister through this entire experience. You are truly a blessing in this world. I couldn't recommend Nathan and Stacia more. They are Sound and the Furry: www.soundandthefurry.com.

I am grateful to the many brilliant artists and industry professionals whose voices I got to weave into my book (in no particular order): Alex Lacamoire, Alex Timbers, Alaine Alldaffer, Burt Bacharach, Rob Meffe, Michael Minarik, Cindi Rush, Carrie Gardner, Stephen Kopel, Bernie Telsey, Stephanie Klapper, Gayle Seay, Scott Wojcik, Michael Mayer, Jay Binder, VP Boyle, Jen Waldman, Carmel Dean, Andrew Zerman, Geoff Johnson, Andy Blankenbuehler, Adam Wachter, Dave Clemmons,

Eddie Rabin, Donell Foreman, Anthony Lee Medina, Kerry Butler, Larry O'Keefe, Stephen Oremus, Michael McElroy, Tom Kitt, Tom Burke, Mark Blankenship, Elizabeth Ziff, and Paula Murray Cole.

To the theater community, which I'm so blessed to be part of, thank you for believing in me.

To all my students, thank you for making me a great teacher!

A very special thanks to my book consultant Stephanie Gunning.

Thank you to my editor Bernadette Malavarca for being so good at what she does!

And finally, Rusty Cutchin, thanks for saying yes to a really great idea I had!

www.asteponline.org

ASTEP is a nonprofit organization that uses the arts as a method of teaching HIV education and life skills to children living in extreme poverty around the globe.

Introduction

The way my relationship with rock music or, more specifically, with music from "off the radio" began has everything to do with my mother. When I was fourteen, my mother lost both of her parents within a few months of each other. She is an emotional woman, as am I, and she had a terrible time when her parents were sick because she was an only child, and her parents were really old and needed all of her time and attention. She ran them to this doctor and that doctor, back and forth to and from the hospital . . . for years.

I was always with her.

We'd be driving along in her Buick Skylark, listening to 106.7 Lite FM, when a song would come on, and she'd scream, "Oh my God! 'I've Never Been to Me'! Charlene sang that! It was 1982, I was separated from your father, and dating Elliot, the cookie maker." Then she would sing along, off-key, "I've been to paradise, but I've never been to meeeeeeeee," and begin weeping about certain events that took place during her life.

Weeping went on to the accompaniment of some of my mother's favorite songs, which included Whitney Houston's "The Greatest Love of All," Little River Band's "Reminiscing," Barbra Streisand's "Run Wild," "You're a Native New Yorker" by Odyssey, Patty Austin and James Ingram's "Baby, Come to Me," Jerry Rafferty's "Baker Street," and "Swearin' to God" by the Four Seasons. My mother associated all of her feelings and life experiences with popular music.

While all this was happening in the car, I'd roll my eyes and think, "Oh Mommy, you're so dramatic!" But secretly, I grew to really love these songs, and to love the feelings that they evoked in my mother . . . and in me.

I know now that experiencing the way my mother's spirits got lifted in that car when she heard disco, the deep pain she felt when she realized things about herself, and every feeling in between, was not only a privilege, it was also the key to my future career.

Soon *I* became an adult, too, and began having my own feelings ...and lots of them. There were great songs on the radio that took me to the heart of my emotions, just like my mother was taken. "Oh Me, Oh My" would come on, and it was, "Oh! That's Aretha Franklin! Ohhh ...I was nineteen years old...," and now I'd be the one weeping at the memory of my first love and the ache that *still* remained, even years later. The song meant something to me. It had my emotions in it. It was like a bookmark in my history and my sense of self.

As a musical theater performer, I decided to audition for rock musicals like *Rent*, *The Full Monty*, and *Aida*, with "Oh Me, Oh My." I got called back for so many rock musicals, and I booked acting work like a madwoman . . . for *years*. The creative teams of these productions responded to me *so* beautifully when I'd sing that song. They thought I was clever, poetic, funny, honest, and inspired.

So, then I applied my ability to interpret music with my own unique point of view to my legit musical theater auditions, and I had the same success. I booked tons of legit musicals and played diverse roles, such as a loony maid in turn-of-the-century England and an Amish Girl. I've played two birds, a bear, a muskrat, and a squirrel. I've been a puppeteer. I played a revolutionary Jew living on the Lower East Side of Manhattan during the Depression. I starred in an opera based on the murder of Kitty Genovese. I played Little Becky in the National Tour of the Broadway musical *Urinetown*. And I've done lots of other characters in between.

All of these successes came from a girl who loves to listen to the radio.

Now, all those songwriters did not write their songs about my feelings; they wrote about theirs. But I interpreted their lyrics and music through the filter of who I am, how I see things, and infused them with *my* history, *my* feelings. That's how I sang all of them so well.

In 2005, I fell in love with Amy Rogers, Director of the Musical Theater Program at Pace University. Though we are no longer in a relationship, we remain dear friends, and I hold her in the highest regard. She is a visionary who trains her students to be open, unique, and creative team players with a phenomenal work ethic. The first time Amy heard me sing rock music was at a concert I did with a bunch of friends in the basement of the Drama Book Shop. After the concert, she said, "Sheri, you need to teach other performers how to do that!" Reflexively, I said "*No* way! This technique is *mine*."

As our relationship progressed, Amy noticed what life was like for me as an actress. When I was working, I felt amazing. When given the opportunity, my acting was groundbreaking. When I was out of work in the theater and waiting on tables, I felt like I was worthless, as if I had no value. All I ever wanted to do, as an actress, was to change people's lives. When I couldn't do that, I would become self-destructive. I'd have nowhere to put my feelings. I'd ruin things and subsequently have to do an exceptional amount of damage control. Ever loving, Amy turned to me and said, "No, Sheri. You need to teach. You need to focus your emotional energy outwards when you are not onstage."

In an inspired move, Amy set up a class for me at Pace University. Not knowing what it would be like, I walked into the room with a bit of resistance. I didn't *want* to be a teacher. I didn't *want* to give up acting. She had me listen to her class of juniors sing their legit musical theater audition songs. Then I picked out favorite rock tunes that I thought would sound good on their voices, and I taught them how to perform them. I picked great songs like Olivia Newton-John's "Have You Never Been Mellow?," Stevie Wonder's "Overjoyed," "Your Smiling Face" by James Taylor, "You're No Good" by Linda Ronstadt, and "Come Sail Away" by Styx.

Then I taught Amy's students how to feel the music in their souls and share who they really are, as a gift. I was hooked. I realized then that not only should I share my gift of interpretation for my *own* wellness, but also that Amy was on to something. Not *only* could I could change people's lives, but I could change the face of musical theater—and this was how.

What Amy had recognized is that rock musicals are *dominating* musical theater. This phenomenon has been happening for years, and will continue for years to come.

All rock musical auditions *require* actors to sing a song that comes "off the radio." If you walked in with a musical theater song, even one drawn from the score of a rock musical, you would appear unprofessional and ill prepared.

So, here *you* are, left to ask yourself, "But how on earth do I do this? I don't know any rock songs. I've been listening to musical theater show tunes my whole life. I have *no* training in rock music *whatsoever*—no one trained us in school for that!" You must figure out how to succeed in a genre of musical theater that you know next to nothing about. Thus, I bring you *Rock the Audition*.

By the end of this book, you will be able to:

▶ Pick your own exciting songs that already have, or have room to create, a dramatic arc.

▶ Create your own appropriate cuts and arrangements, and successfully communicate the feel of the song to a pianist who only knows how to play legit musical theater music.

▶ Have a keen understanding of the world in which the musical you are auditioning for takes place, and what that means about the way you need to perform your song in order to capture the essence of that time period.

▶Recognize how best to handle the different vocal styles of each generation, and see the details of how styles changed and grew throughout time.

▶Interpret the meaning of what the original recording artists were saying through these songs.

▶Learn how to act a rock song.

▶Be clear on what your physical expression in the audition room needs to be when singing a rock song (the requirements are profoundly different than those in a legit musical theater audition).

▶Bring who you are and your own unique point of view to these interpretations.

You see, this is the gift of music or any great art form for that matter. It is open for interpretation! You have a golden opportunity when you sing a rock song. You get to create a character based on what the song means to you, not based on a character that already exists.

When auditioning for classical musical theater, the song you choose to sing has a clear story in it. It is meant to move an already existing plot along because it is from a musical in which each song is a piece of a bigger puzzle. When auditioning for a rock musical, your rock song won't be connected to a preexisting story. It *is* the story! It is a moment in time that stands on its own! You get to make this story anything you choose, based upon how you interpret it! The interpretation of a rock song is in your hands.

So I dare you, dear performer, to turn the page and become the brilliant *rock star* you were always meant to be.

A Note on Using the DVD and Book

The DVD enclosed at the back of the book includes video demonstrations that you will watch at intervals while reading *Rock the Audition*. Some are on vocal techniques, some are on physical mannerisms and illustrate how to move your body, and some are a synthesis of the vocals, body, and interpretations of the text of the song.

As you become familiar with the various tracks, you will find that you are able to go directly to the voice, body, and interpretation tracks that will help you synthesize a well-rounded performance before an audition for a pop or rock musical set in any time period.

A directive in the text indicates when to watch specific tracks. The first such instruction occurs in Chapter 6.

1

What Is Expected of Me?

L isten. Rock songs were never intended to be acted. We were meant to dance to them, work out to them, make sweet love to them, and sing them in the shower or while we are wasted at a karaoke bar, but we were certainly not meant to act them.

Popular music, in its truest form, goes verse–chorus—verse–chorus—bridge–chorus. How can you possibly tell a story when it goes back and forth like that? And how on earth are you supposed to act the "repeat-and-fade" that's written at the end of a song anyway—get quieter as you walk away from your audition spot and move toward the door?

Yet here we are today, entirely responsible for picking a great rock song off the radio, creating the perfect audition cut from it (one that has a killer storytelling arc), styling the music vocally, and acting that song with no help at all. Not one bit. This is a *wildly* different way to prepare and perform than is expected from us in a legit musical theater audition. In musical theater, "legit" (which is shorthand for "legitimate") means that a production features songs genuinely written for the stage and designed for theatrical storytelling.

Casting directors at a legit audition insist on singers performing songs that were specifically written for a musical. Why? These songs have perfect dramatic arcs *already* built into them, because they are from musicals where the plot is developed through the lyrics. But with a rock musical audition, the song a singer has to sing isn't connected to an already existing story. Again, it's not from a musical. It's a track off a popular artist's CD.

Knowing that we are expected to do these things on our own, we either don't go to a given rock musical audition because we are afraid we are going to fail miserably at it, or we decide to go and then feel wretched and self-conscious the whole time we are auditioning because we don't know if what we are doing is what the producers and casting directors are looking for. Unless we are represented by an agent or a talent manager, we rarely get feedback. The only way we know if we've been successful at an audition is if we get a callback.

By choosing to read this book, you are taking your life and career into your own hands. What do you get for being so brave? You get a chance to learn what the directors, casting directors, musical directors, composers, and choreographers of the hottest rock musicals on Broadway so desperately want you to know! *Rock the Audition* will radically demystify the rock musical audition for you—from preparation through performance—empowering you to succeed in ways you never dreamed possible.

Before I teach you how to rock your next audition, let me give you the Sheri Sanders *Readers Digest* version of the history of rock musicals. You have *got* to understand why and in what specific ways musical theater auditions have so drastically changed. Fasten your seatbelt. You are about to take a fast and furious ride!

"Back in the Day"

Did you know that back in the day, many of the big hits on the radio *came* from the scores of musicals? For example, "Summertime" by composer George Gershwin and lyricist DuBose Heyward came from their 1935 opera *Porgy and Bess*. The standard "My Funny Valentine" by composer Richard Rodgers and lyricist Lorenz Hart came from their 1937 musical *Babes in Arms*. "All the Things You Are" by composer Jerome Kern and lyricist Oscar Hammerstein II came from their 1939 musical *Very Warm for May*. These songs became the popular, or "pop," tunes of their era.

Rob Meffe, Director of Music at Pace University, informs me: "The truth is that Rodgers and Kern and Berlin were all trying to write pop songs and the songs they wrote were many times shoehorned into different Broadway musicals, revues, and films until they found their place. It really wasn't until the 1940s with the rise of *Oklahoma!* and shows like it that Broadway writers were tailoring their songs to fit the context of character, situation and plot."[1]

Rock Musicals in the '60s and '70s

In 1960, *Bye Bye Birdie* with music by Charles Strouse and lyrics by Lee Adams was a hit on Broadway. Although Conrad Birdie, the lead character, is based on Elvis Presley, the songs in the show are not rock songs. Rob Meffe adds: "By any definition, *Birdie* would not be considered a rock musical. Strouse's music did, however, incorporate some of the nonsense lyrics and rhythmic feel of Presley's earlier works, but no one in the audience thought for a moment that they were there to hear genuine rock music. If anything, *Birdie* is a satiric look at the celebrity excesses of the rock movement."[2] Even though there really was no such thing as a "rock musical" back then, this was the twinkle in the eye of what would eventually be the birth of the rock musical genre.

Then things changed. In 1968, renowned composer, lyricist, and singer Burt Bacharach, along with his songwriting partner Hal David, wrote the music and lyrics for the Broadway hit *Promises, Promises*, adapted by playwright Neil Simon from the screenplay of the Oscar-winning movie *The Apartment.* This musical comedy was a breakthrough in the category of the "pop" musical because it was the first time a composer of pop songs wrote a musical that perfectly captured the changing sound of authentic radio hits as we know them.

Bacharach, the composer of *Promises, Promises,* by contrast, started his musical career writing songs in the Brill Building. The Brill Building was the creative epicenter of the music industry. It was an office building in midtown Manhattan where some of the top songwriters of the twenty-first century honed their craft in the early days of their careers. Among them were pivotal, music-changing artists such as Carole King, Ellie Greenwich, Laura Nyro, Jerry Leiber, Mike Stoller, Barry Mann, Cynthia Weil, Neil Sedaka, Paul Simon, and Phil Spector, to name only a few. Please look up the works of these unbelievable songwriters, as they will become an incredible source of audition material for you. Bacharach wrote fantastic, memorable songs made famous by the greatest pop artists of the 1960s and 1970s, singers who include, among others, Dusty Springfield, Aretha Franklin, the Shirelles, Dionne Warwick, the Drifters, Tom Jones, and the Beatles. Bacharach and Hal David took their skills and wrote an authentic 1960s pop musical.

Get a load of this: *Promises, Promises* was considered legit musical theater despite its composer being a popular songwriter. So even with all of his own unforgettable tunes, like the hits "Walk on By," "You'll Never Get to Heaven (If You Break My Heart)," "What the World Needs Now," "(There's) Always Something There to Remind Me," and "Wishin' and Hopin'" available to them, the actors auditioning didn't make the connection between his radio hits and his musical score. According to Bacharach, whom I interviewed for this book, "Even though there was sheet music available for my songs, performers didn't think to sing them in order to book the job. They auditioned for the production with legit musical theater songs."[3]

At the same time as audiences were being delighted by the sweet-hearted pop musical *Promises, Promises, Hair* was rocking the Broadway stage. In 1967, *Hair* dared conservative audiences to abandon everything they knew about musical theater. It insisted on taking them on a wild ride that was both evolutionary and revolutionary. Nobody dreamed that rock and roll would ever exist on the stage in a dramatic way.

Elizabeth L. Wollman, author of *The Theatre Will Rock* (University of Michigan Press 2006), describes the casting of *Hair*, quoting the director, Tom O'Horgan, "During the audition period, Ragni, Rado, MacDermot [the creative team], and I were less interested in professionalism than we were in finding actors who could interpret the material realistically. 'We were looking for the real thing,' O'Horgan says, 'but the kids who did it at the Public were like glossy print kids— regular kids that they dressed up like hippies. It was pretty awful.'"[4] *Hair* was the inaugural musical production at Joseph Papp's Public Theater in 1967, an Off-Broadway venue in Greenwich Village.

Much of the difficulty of producing *Hair* lay in finding actors who could sing rock music convincingly. According to Wollman, a number of the actors who appeared in *Hair* remember auditioning with rock songs, a practice that was *unheard of* on Broadway at that time. It is hard to believe that the idea of singing songs off the radio *never* caught on during this revolutionary era, which birthed the rock musical.

Despite such outrageous and innovative musicals as Andrew Lloyd Webber's *Jesus Christ Superstar,* Galt MacDermot's *Two Gentlemen of Verona,* and three Stephen Schwartz productions running on Broadway at the same time—*Godspell, Pippin,* and *The Magic Show* (not to mention the tuneful 1950s rock and roll musical *Grease*)—actors didn't sing songs from their favorite radio stations.

Just as these great musicals were rocking our socks off...uh-oh... a bunch of failed rock musicals also got produced, shows like *Dude, Soon, Via Galactica, Ain't Supposed to Die a Natural Death,* and *Man on the Moon*, which tried desperately (to no avail) to follow in the footsteps of the more successful *Hair*. Unfortunately for their creative teams, these shows flopped. And it did not go unnoticed. Both music scholars and theater writers predicted the demise of the rock musical. Wollman says, "This string of failures helped convince many members of New York's theater industry that with few exceptions, a successful rock musical was a contradiction in terms. As the number of rock musical fatalities climbed, producers grew wary of anything billed as a 'rock musical' or a 'rock opera' and the appearance of such properties on Broadway diminished significantly."[5]

In other words, times were tough for our friend, the rock musical.

Meanwhile, across the pond in London, Andrew Lloyd Webber was achieving such success with the rock opera *Jesus Christ Superstar* that he decided to bring it to Broadway in 1971. In 1976, he followed it up in London with a second rock opera, *Evita,* the story of Eva Perón, wife of Argentine dictator Juan Perón, which was also a smash hit on Broadway in 1979. So despite the "death of the rock musical" in the United States, Webber continued honing innovative new concepts for rock-based shows.

Andrew Lloyd Webber and the Mega-Musical Movement of the '80s

In the mid-1980s, after great labor, Lloyd Webber gently rebirthed the rock musical. He delivered a big, big baby, the theatrical phenomenon we now call the mega-musical. With "mega" being the second child of the rock musical movement, it has been much easier for audiences to handle—so easy, in fact, that the kid is still kicking around today.

The Phantom of the Opera, of course, is the greatest example of Lloyd Webber's mega-musical movement because it has been running since 1986. But *Cats,* which was produced on the West End in London in 1981 and Broadway in 1982, was the first of his many pop mega-musicals, and it was immediately joined on Broadway by *Joseph and the Amazing Technicolor Dreamcoat* in 1982. Decca Records had originally recorded the score as a concept album in 1969. *Song and Dance* opened in London in 1982 and then in New York in 1985, and *Starlight Express* played in the West End in 1984 and on Broadway in 1987. Each of Lloyd Webber's pop musicals is as splashy and dramatic as a rock concert, but with a Lite-FM soundtrack.

Claude-Michel Schönberg was the other well-known mega-musical composer of the time, responsible for the creation of *Les Miserables* (London 1985, Broadway 1987) and *Miss Saigon* (London 1989, Broadway 1991). In particular, what he and Lloyd Webber tapped into was an approachable musical style that was integrated into grand settings and epic operatic stories. So ticket buyers who did not want to see an actual "high-brow" opera could plunk their money down and get "culture" in the form of *The Phantom of the Opera.* After all, who wants to sit through three hours of the opera *Turandot* just to hear the aria "Nessun Dorma"? The mega-musical is marketing genius.

The common denominator of all mega-musicals is their gigantic production value. However, musically, their style goes all over the place. *Phantom of the Opera, Chess* (lyrics by Tim Rice, and music written by Bjorn Ulvaeus and Benny Andersson formerly of the group ABBA), and *Les Miserables* couldn't sound more different. There is not one consistent "mega-musical sound."

What casting directors and the creative teams were looking for when they were auditioning performers for these productions was as contemporary a sound as possible. Performing a legit musical theater song with a pop/rock influence, such as a song by Lloyd Webber or Schönberg, was absolutely an appropriate choice.

To quote Andrew Zerman, who collaborated on casting several mega-musicals in the United States in the 1980s with Johnson/Liff Casting, "No one asked for a rock song off the radio because rock songs are not inherently 'actable pieces.' If you happened to have one, they loved to hear it, but it needed to be a song by someone like Billy Joel, who has inherent storytelling ability. It was only for the production of *Dreamgirls*," says Zerman, "that we distinctly asked for Motown, R&B, and soul." [6]

A New Vocal Trend in the '80s

Three amazing singers—Liz Callaway, who sang "The Story Goes On" in *Baby;* Betty Buckley, who sang "Memory" in *Cats;* and Frances Ruffelle, who sang "On My Own" in *Les Miserables*—changed *everything* about the way people sang musical theater. When our emotions grew bigger, we started singing higher, and suddenly we were in the land of "high belting." I learned how to sing pop musical theater by studying the emotional expressiveness of these singers.

Richard Maltby Jr., director and co-lyricist (with Don Black) of Andrew Lloyd Webber's production *Song and Dance* and co-lyricist of Schönberg's *Miss Saigon*, formed an ideal partnership with composer David Shire to create the pop musical *Baby* (Broadway1983). Shire, coincidentally, wrote my favorite duet (with lyrics by Carol Connors) of all time, "With You I'm Born Again," which was an international chart hit sung by Billy Preston and Syreeta. He won the Academy Award for Best Song (with Norman Gimbel) for the theme song to the movie *Norma Rae,* "It Goes Like It Goes," and was also nominated for two Grammy Awards for great disco tunes he wrote for the soundtrack to *Saturday Night Fever.* Prior to *Baby,* Maltby and Shire had written *Starting Here, Starting Now* (1977). Later they would write *Closer Than Ever* (1989). Of their three collaborations, *Baby* was the musical that helped put the pop sound on the musical theater map, despite it being a simple show about three couples and their personal struggles to have babies.

Claude-Michel Schönberg deliberately wrote lines in *Les Miserables* that were on a woman's passaggio (the place where the vocal break between registers exists). He felt *this* area of the vocal range, where the voice is on the verge of cracking, was the most vulnerable and exciting part of a woman's voice. True fact: Claude-Michel had Cyndi Lauper's voice on his mind when he wrote "On My Own."

It's ironic that nowadays female singers are expected to make the jump *over* their passaggio effortlessly, because a seamless transition from the low to the high vocal range actually defeats Claude-Michel's intention.

According to Stephen Oremus, original music director and music supervisor of *Wicked,*

> In the '80s, music directors were saying, "Okay, now you have to be able to hit an E like it's nothing," and when *Wicked* came along, now it's "Okay, now you have to hit an F like it's nothing—and also make it sound more pop/rock while you do." Your voice must have a real fluidity in the sound. This is especially true for women's voices. You know you've got that danger zone of B flat to D where singers are either going to mix their way through it and fool you into thinking they can belt it all, or they're going to have a big hole in their voice. It's less about what notes they are going to hit and more about how they navigate through the passaggio to get there. But it's not about simply reaching a note anyway. It's how you get there and what kind of colors that note can have when you do.[7]

The Emergence of the New Rock Musical in the 1990s

In 1992, *Tommy,* a musical based on the concept album by the rock group the Who, rocked the Broadway stage. Casting for this production was perhaps the first time anyone suggested that performers prepare a rock song off the radio for their audition. According to Michael McElroy, an actor in the original production, because he had no rock songs in his repertoire, he quickly learned "Get Back" by the Beatles.

It was *Rent* (written and composed by Jonathan Larson) that not only changed the face of contemporary musical theater when it opened on Broadway in 1996, but also completely transformed the audition process. *Rent* was the first musical for which the creative team *insisted* that actors sing a song taken off the radio at their auditions.

Bernie Telsey started his career as a casting director for the original Off-Broadway production, and then became a celebrated casting director through its rise to musical theater superstardom, founding the casting agency Telsey and Company in the process. *Rent* was nominated for ten Tony Awards, won four (including Best Musical), and garnered a Pulitzer Prize for drama. "People didn't even know what 'singing a rock song' meant," Telsey told me. "When we said that we have to hear an actual song off the radio, people said, 'You mean it's okay to do an Aretha Franklin song?' 'Yes.' 'Really?' 'Yes! You can sing whatever you want as long as it's off the radio.' But they brought in a legit song and tried to rock out with it. *Rent* was so much about 'you being who you are' that we didn't demand people act music like you would a legit song. The idea our director, Michael Greif, had, was that 'we will create Maureen or Mimi around you.'"[8]

Rent was the first show in the history of musical theater that a casting office opened the audition process up to the actual rock community. As Telsey says,

> We wanted real authentic rock singers. We went out to clubs; we listened to bands. It was so hard to find that quality in contemporary musical theater performers. We saw every actor in the musical theater community, and couldn't find this real rock sound, so we looked outside. It was easier to find a rock singer and teach them how to connect emotionally than to get a musical theater person to rock out, so we had auditions all over the country. We had to . . . At one point we had to simultaneously cast five touring companies of *Rent*.
>
> Our calls were open to everyone who wanted to sing. They brought people out from the woodwork. Wherever we went there were a thousand people there. It was very much like *American Idol* auditions are today. We really found great people. They were authentic. That's what the show was about.[9]

Along with the massive success of this production both on Broadway and in subsequent touring productions came the necessity to learn rock songs for the purpose of auditioning. You were now required to be expressive and theatrical within an entirely different framework. And that framework is the stories that rock singers tell.

Frank Wildhorn: Pop Musicals with an Edge

While all the rock music madness of *Rent* was occurring, audiences were also being introduced to the lavish pop musicals of composer Frank Wildhorn, productions such as *The Scarlet Pimpernel* (1997), *Jekyll and Hyde* (1997), and *The Civil War* (1998). In 1998, he was the first American composer since Stephen Schwartz to have had three shows running on Broadway simultaneously. Here's a little-known tidbit about Mr. Wildhorn. Did you know that he wrote pop music for Whitney Houston in the '80s? Yes, he sure did. Among other well-known songs, he wrote "Where Do Broken Hearts Go?"

Dave Clemmons has been the primary casting director for Wildhorn Productions, for which he handled casting on the National Tour of *Jekyll and Hyde, The Civil War,* and *Wonderland* (Broadway opening April 2011). In interviewing Dave for this book, he told me that when he is casting for Wildhorn, he is looking for a performer who has "dynamic vocals and the emotional capacity to match. Linda Eder, a primary vocalist for Wildhorn's pop musicals, is a perfect example of that synthesis."[10] Pop music from the late '80s coincidentally allows both of these dimensions of a performance to exist.

An Interview with Casting Director Dave Clemmons

Sheri: For the tour of *Jekyll and Hyde*, Frank Wildhorn was looking for a broad sound and performance. But you didn't request a pop song although it was a pop musical.

Dave: The *Jekyll* score is so theatrical. Yes, there is a pop form to a lot of the music, but it's theatricality with a pop edge. Frank wanted people who could approximate that style when it was called for in the score: theatrically dynamic with a pop sensibility. So we didn't need a pop song, just a pop sound. It wasn't until *The Civil War,* which was my first casting gig ever, that we specifically asked for pop, rock, and R&B tunes. I remember listing at least twenty pop singers for performers to choose from, including Stevie Wonder, Whitney Houston, Faith Hill, and George Michael. We knew there was sheet music available for the music of all these great singers.

Sheri: All the names you mentioned are dramatic singers with voices that have a huge vocal range. So, what you are saying is that you led the horses to water . . . .

Dave: But nobody drank. Right! Despite our instructions, people still came in with legit musical theater selections for their auditions.

Sheri: That great idea to sing pop music didn't stick at all with the performers?

Dave: No, it didn't stick!

Sheri: You've cast every possible kind of rock musical: *The Civil War, Bat Boy, Bare, Brooklyn,* and *Jesus Christ Superstar.* For auditions, casting directors ask performers to "bring in a pop/rock tune," and it leaves them feeling lost. With all the different styles of rock musicals, this request seems general.

Dave: I can tell you one thing right there. We know better than to try to be specific. I can't say bring in a 1970s rock song, as people won't have it. We're lucky if people know *any* sort of a rock song. I'll accept *anything* off of the radio. People don't put different styles of pop/rock in their audition books. We're lucky if they have *one*, so we have to be general. We have to be that general in order for you to show me that you can be non-theatrical sounding and access *any* sort of pop, rock, country, or R&B style. I'll take *anything* to do that. I *wish* I could be more specific and say what kind of song, but I know that people just don't have it.

Your Rock Musical Audition Book

Over the years, the rock musical has taken on many different forms, each with its own profoundly different storytelling style. Consider the genres of music in a handful of shows produced on and Off-Broadway since *Bye Bye Birdie. Dreamgirls* (1981), which is set in the 1960s, features early Motown. *The Wedding Singer* (2006) features 1980s pop. *Spring Awakening* (2007) features contemporary alternative folk/rock. *Billy Elliot* (2008) features contemporary pop written by Elton John. *Bloody Bloody Andrew Jackson* (2010) is "emo" rock.

Are you getting what I'm saying, people? One song does *not* cut it for *all* your rock musical auditions.

If you audition for any of the aforementioned musicals, whether the production is a revival or regional, and even if it is an original production of a play having its first run on or off Broadway, you *will* be asked to sing a tune of some kind off of the radio that is musically appropriate for your audition. For your legit musical theater auditions, you have your trusty three-ring binder with all of your necessary audition material in it: a Broadway standard (that's what "My Funny Valentine" is considered), a Golden Age up-tempo song and ballad (anything from *Oklahoma* through 1970), a mid-century up-tempo and ballad (1970–1980), and a contemporary up-tempo and ballad. You must open your mind to the idea that along with your legit song selections, your "audition book" *must* have as extensive a repertoire of pop/rock tunes as your legit material.

Bernie Telsey says,

I think, while *Rent* changed the face of musical theater, it set up a habit of people being non-specific. *Rent* said to people, "I don't want a character. I want you, your soul and your style, in every way." We were asking for people to be who they were, and not "play a character," but we still asked people to connect emotionally to the song. I don't know where that connection went or why it didn't stay. Actors come in now, knowing they have to sing a rock song, and they'll sing "Think" by Aretha Franklin, but they don't realize they have to tell a story. Although they *have* to connect to the song to be successful in an audition, they don't. I guess that's the stinky part about *American Idol.* People started coming in and screaming. We're taking it for granted now.

Where I think the influence of *American Idol* is advantageous, on the other hand, is that when they get down to the final twelve performers, they have to interpret all sorts of different styles. This demonstrates how specific you have to be . . . and it shows that you have to be really good at them all. The contestants have to come in every week and master a style. It also shows that it takes a whole week to work on a song, and how truly necessary preparation is.[11]

A Roundtable Discussion with the Roundabout Theatre Company/Jim Carnahan Casting

Remember when I said to fasten your seatbelt? Now I need you to tighten it.

While writing this book, I sat in on a number of Equity principal auditions (EPA) and Equity chorus calls (ECC). If you are a newbie to the theater world, Actors' Equity is the onstage performers' union, which regulates how actors are treated and how much access we have to auditions. Once you earn an "Equity card" (membership), you have the right to go to EPAs and ECCs to audition. In an EPA, you will be seen by a casting person from the office of the show for which you are auditioning. At an ECC, you will be seen by a casting person (like Dave Clemmons or someone from Telsey and Company) and someone from the creative team (the producer, director, or musical director).

Anyway, I sat in on these auditions for several Broadway and Off-Broadway shows, and I saw that an actor's entire preparation process was very evident in the way the actor auditioned. This is what I saw over and over again: Someone had told the actor about the casting call the day before, and he or she thought, "Shit, I need a rock song! Oh what was that song . . . ? 'I'm with You' by Avril Lavigne! That'll show me off." And then the actor ran the song in his or her head, sang it in the shower the night before, pictured how he or she would do it in the audition, showed up at the Equity Building in Times Square at 6 a.m. to get an appointment at 9 a.m. for later in the day, ran over to Colony Records to pick up "the big book of the world's greatest rock balladz," came back to the audition, waited, then put that big book on the piano with no cuts marked in the music, having never ever sung through it with a piano player to even see if it's in the right key. As the piano player was playing with one hand and trying to keep the book (which had never been opened before) open with the other . . . *and* trying to turn the pages, guess what happened? The fantasy rock star performance turned into the greatest shit show on earth. I saw that same scenario repeated by different performers all day long. One of the casting calls where I saw this happen consistently was at the auditions for *American Idiot.*

I met with casting directors Stephen Kopel and Carrie Gardner, who work for the Roundabout Theatre Company.[12] They cast *Spring Awakening, American Idiot,* and *Bloody Bloody Andrew Jackson.* We started our conversation by discussing the problems they commonly experience in auditions.

Carrie: The number one problem we encounter when auditioning for a rock musical is song choice. Many musical theater actors only have one song "rock" song in their audition book, and sing it for every audition. "Alone" by Heart is a particular favorite.

Stephen: Or "I'm with You" by Avril Lavigne.

Sheri: When I sat in on your *American Idiot* auditions, it was "Somebody to Love" by Queen.

Stephen: For more traditional musical theater auditions, actors usually work on a song with an acting coach and a voice teacher. When they are auditioning for a rock musical, there is often a disconnect that happens. They don't feel that they need to prepare as thoroughly.

Carrie: In the early days of *American Idiot,* no one came in with a Green Day song.

Sheri: Even though it is a Green Day musical? That's shocking!

Carrie: What it boils down to is a lack of preparation, or misguided preparation. It's important that when you are auditioning for a new musical like *American Idiot* you find out everything you can about the show and prepare accordingly. *American Idiot* obviously has a score by Green Day, so it's essential that you prepare material that makes sense in that world. A song by Lady Gaga or Kid Rock doesn't work. Not all rock songs are created equal, and just because a song is considered rock it doesn't necessarily work for every audition. You can't have one universal rock song in your book. I did a day of auditions for *American Idiot,* and I invited actors to audition who I wouldn't normally consider putting into a rock musical. I figured this was their opportunity to make us think of them in a different way, as they aren't given this opportunity very often. All they had to do was sing a rock song. That's it. An appropriate rock song.

Stephen: But they came in and took a rock song and turned it into a musical theater song. A rock song (at least in an audition setting) is all about creating a mood or a feeling. It's about living in the song. You can't act a rock song in the same way you act a musical theater song. If you treat them in the same way, the results are often (unintentionally) hilarious. Auditioning well is about knowing *how* to prepare.

Many actors don't do their homework. People get an audition for a Broadway musical. They go to their audition book (still full of their repertoire from college) and pick a song they think will work. If that's all the effort you're going to put into your audition, why bother?

Carrie: We give actors *days* to prepare a song. No sides. All they have to do is sing one song. But many of them still don't even listen to the album.

Stephen: I'm here, rooting for you, really wanting you to succeed . . .

Sheri: Yes, and they are failing you. You want them to be great. You want to give them their big break.

Carrie: Exactly. You want someone to walk in the room and be perfect. We want you to be the answer to our casting problem. Non-Equity actors are a great example of actors preparing in the wrong way. They wait for hours and hours to get in, sitting outside the audition room all day long hoping for a chance to be seen. They think, "The more auditions, the better." They think they are doing their job by showing up on that day, as if this is a numbers game. "How many auditions can I get to in a week?" and "Look how committed I am" and "I got in the door." But when they get in the door, they use the same overdone song they use for every other audition. I'm thinking, "You've been sitting here *all* day. You've been hearing other people sing *all* day. You've had time to think about this!"

Sheri: I think their persistence is amazing, and necessary since this is really the only way a non-Equity actor could get seen to book a job. What isn't good is that on top of their dedication they aren't self-aware. But there has been no formal training in auditioning for rock musicals. So people just have no idea how they need to show up.

Carrie: That's true. Women in particular have a misconception that they need to blow you out of the room with their song. And nothing is more tiresome than listening to someone scream a song at you for two minutes. It's our job to find out if you can sing that high note, but first, please, let us get interested in you as a person.

Stephen: Totally. I want to know what you're all about. I want to know who you are, and what your point of view is, not how high you can scream.

Carrie: I mean . . . we're casting *American Idiot, Spring Awakening.* I am not concerned about how high you can sing.

These shows aren't about belting as high as you can. It's obvious from listening to the cast albums, or to a Duncan Sheik album or to any of Green Day's albums. These shows are about emotionally connected singing.

Sheri: I think it boils down to competitiveness. They feel, "I have to riff higher and sing louder to be better than anyone else."

Stephen: I totally understand that thinking; it's just not true. Ultimately, we just want to like you. If we like you, we'll spend as much time as we need to in the audition room figuring out if you have the high notes. Engage us. Let us see your unique take on your song. When an actor walks into the room and engages you with a simple, quiet ballad, it's refreshing. I can't stress that enough. We really want to know who you are and what makes you special. I think a big problem is that people haven't thought enough about who they are and what unique things they bring into the audition room that no one else does. They just put up their "performer façade." We want to see the person... the human being, not an auditioning robot.

Carrie: Especially at a general like an EPA or an ECC. You are not a character in that moment. Show us what makes you special, what makes you different from the other 300 people we've already seen that day.

Sheri: The funny thing is that I feel like singing rock music is liberating.

Stephen: It should be. But that freedom is often why people crash and burn. It's too big, too open. Actors don't know how to handle it. For me there is nothing better than an actor who walks in the room with confidence and shows us how they approach this specific type of material. It's as simple as that.

Carrie: I think actors lack a basic understanding of auditioning and the business side of things in general. Many of them are not properly prepared to be competitive in this challenging climate. When you're auditioning for a Broadway musical, everyone sings and acts well. That's already a given. It's the details that are important. It's the ability to be very specific and very simple at the same time. When you graduate from college, your preparation for the business is often your professor telling you to wear this little audition dress . . .

Stephen: . . . and never stop smiling.

Sheri: No one cultivates a person's originality. People are told what roles they're right for.

Carrie: We go to senior showcases at these colleges, and we feel like we are on a cruise ship.

Stephen: It's actor after actor singing as loud and as high as they can with a fake smile plastered on their face. They're trying *so* hard, but there's not an emotionally interesting moment anywhere.

Carrie: We need you to connect to the material. Just think about what you are singing while you are singing it. It makes all the difference in the world. There's a common problem we call dead eyes. It sounds worse than it is.

Stephen: No, it's terrible, actually.

Carrie: It's so clear when an actor is not connected to what they are singing. It's all in the eyes. Ultimately, I don't care about how you sound. Be in the moment. The ability to be alive in a song makes all the difference in the world.

Stephen: It's all about researching the piece and figuring out how you fit into that world.

Sheri: So you would say, "Do your homework. Show care, be detailed, and keep it simple. And be yourself."

Stephen: Yes.

Sheri: Carrie, any pearls for the people?

Carrie: It's about working on the things you can control. What's in your audition book? What are you wearing? And what is your attitude like in the room? Your attitude is a huge thing.

Sheri: Attitude toward you?

Carrie: Toward us, toward the accompanist, toward the reader, and toward the experience. How are you treating the people in the room? People come in really angry. They walk in the room angry. They're angry that they have to wait, angry because it's tense and competitive in the waiting room, angry at us because we look too young to be casting directors, angry at the pianist for messing up. All of that stuff turns us right off. If something goes wrong during your audition, handle it like a normal person. If you're terrified and weird, we get uncomfortable. Then there is tension in the room. Everyone messes up, everyone cracks. That doesn't make us write you off. Have a sense of humor about yourself.

Stephen: It's all about the way you conduct yourself in the audition room. The easier going you can be, the better. Bring in good energy. If we get bad vibes from you, there's no way we'll feel comfortable calling you back to be seen by the full creative team, no matter how talented you are.

Carrie: And don't try so hard. Don't do something or say something just for the sake of being remembered. We'll remember, but not necessarily in a good way.

Sheri: Do you want people to adjust their material to the characters or to have them come in as themselves? Should they say this is who I am? This is how I see it? And then you get to decide what role they're right for?

Stephen: Actors are constantly trying to figure out what we want. They are almost always wrong. That's a game you can't win, and you'll make yourself crazy trying. Come in the room, be who you are, and do what you do. And we'll help you every step of the way. We want to help you get this job. And at the end of the day, it's just a job. We're putting on a musical. This is not world peace. As we take notes during auditions, "He's cool" or "He's charming" or "I like him" is some of the highest praise. It's not a life or death situation. Don't treat it like one.

Carrie: Yes. Just be cool. Be a real person so we can feel like real people. We can relax because you are relaxed.

Preparation Is Your Responsibility

Actors need to understand that rock musicals are changing. There's more dialogue . . . more book scenes in them. *Rent* felt like a rock concert with a great story. Now the rock styles are taking the form of legit musical theater shows again. Thus, you must interpret the material, and unless you are auditioning for Stephen Sondheim, you are going to need to know how to interpret a pop/rock song. It's what everyone is asking for.

Bernie Telsey told me,

> I sat with William Finn during our auditions for his new musical, *Little Miss Sunshine.* The music is in the same style as *Falsettos* because it's composed by him. Fifteen years ago, this music would never have been considered pop/rock. Bill's shows have always been considered legit musical theater productions. But because his stories take place in the contemporary world, he decided he would ask actors to do a pop song in their auditions. He wanted to see how people would communicate a pop sensibility, and if this would fit into his mode of storytelling. Literally no one had a pop song for him. This was rather shocking. Actors who have Broadway credits, people who I know are very talented, because I've cast them before, weren't at all prepared.[13]

This is a big problem. If William Finn asks for a pop song at his auditions and his music is considered contemporary musical theater, what are we supposed to sing in an audition for other composers, people like Stephen Schwartz, Andrew Lloyd Webber, and Andrew Lippa? What do we sing for these amazing artists if we want to book a job in one of their musicals? Since musical theater has transformed, and the expectations casting directors place upon us have transformed, we must meet this change with consciousness and bravery. We must take responsibility for being prepared to meet their needs.

With legit musical theater, as a performer, you must fit the mold. What does that mean? We have roles we have been told we should be playing, and this is how we identify ourselves. Basically, we are pigeonholed into certain archetypes. We are told that we are ingenues, sopranos, leading men, lyric baritones, comedic sidekick belters, and character actors. We are told what roles we are right for based on these archetypes into which we fit. We know the shows and know which song to sing to book roles in these shows.

In rock music, however, and in auditioning for rock musicals, *you* are the role. *You* are the character. Rock auditions are about you and the way you interpret the world through *your* eyes. The song is *your* story. It is about *your* life. And so you are entirely responsible for how you choose to be a storyteller within the parameters of the styles that are currently represented on Broadway. Although you can research a composer's past work, there is no single show to rely on when preparing to audition.

So much of the time, our uniqueness gets swallowed up by trying to be right for the role and to fit the mold that we believe producers want us to fit. There is no mold to fit into here, my friend. No conventional characters or archetypes. You are the archetype.

We are here as rock performers to break the mold!

Style and Time Period

Your job as a performer during an audition is to transport the creative team into the world in which the musical takes place. Ultimately, you will do the same for a paying audience, but for now the producers, director, musical director, and casting people are your audience.

If you were auditioning for *Ragtime, 1776, South Pacific, Cabaret, Chicago,* or even *Falsettos,* wouldn't you want to know what was going on in the world during the era in which the musical is set so that you would be authentic and believable in the part you want to portray? My God, I hope so. *Ragtime* is set in the first decade of the twentieth century. *1776* takes place at the beginning of the American Revolution. *Cabaret* is set in Berlin in 1931. *Chicago* is set in the Prohibition. And *Falsettos* is set in the late 1970s in New York City. People conducted themselves differently in each historical era, based on the concerns of their lives.

You have *got* to do the same sort of research in preparation to audition for a role in a rock musical as for a legit musical; in addition to reading the script or libretto, you need to study the time period and the people who inhabit it. Afterwards, you'll have the great opportunity to be creative by making acting choices. My goal for this book is for you to think, "This is what I believe I'd be like if I was living in the world of the 1960s—or the 1970s or 1980s—living under the circumstances of the lives of the people in the story."

This kind of research is a bit like cultural anthropology, the branch of anthropology that studies beliefs, morals, customs, knowledge, art, and habits, and considers how economic and political realities are affecting people's lives. What makes research for a show different than being an anthropologist is that you are looking for insights into the details of your character's behavior that are relevant to the specific story of the musical.

Each decade of rock history is wildly different. Because of this, I am going to give you a delicious taste of what was going on in pop culture during each of the decades since rock music came to be. Why? Because the social trends and the way people lived their lives in these decades should directly influence how you show up in the audition room when you are auditioning for an era-specific show, such as *Jersey Boys* (1950s), *Hair* (1970s), *Rock of Ages* (1980s), and *American Idiot* (2000s), to name a few.

Do Your Homework: Advice from Casting Director Jay Binder

I interviewed Jay Binder, the casting director for the Broadway rock musicals *We Will Rock You, The Times They Are A-Changin',* *The Lion King,* and the Off-Broadway production of *The Marvelous Wonderettes,* as well as a host of spectacularly successful non-rock musical productions.[1] Here's what he had to say about the use of style and time period.

> Some people, when they give an audition, really seem like they are from another time period. Some are naturals at the music of the Golden Age [1900–1950], and their talent lives beautifully in a certain style or era. But most people are not that specific, and they don't know any differently—especially with rock music. The thing is: you have a valuable opportunity. You get to do research and learn very quickly what certain time periods feel like—certain styles— and you can get really good at it. YouTube is the most valuable reference for musical theater performers. It's there that you can study any style of rock music.

Jay also cautions, "Here's the one thing I have no patience for... people who don't try, who don't do their homework, who don't do the research, who don't even think to try. Now, there are some people who just can't capture certain styles that are not natural to them. But if they try, if they do research a style and period, this means something to the creative team and says something great about the performer. It says that they care."

He continues. "A suggestion to you: your song must parallel the show you are auditioning for. For example, when I was casting Bob Dylan's *The Times They Are A-Changin',* actors would come in with the most inappropriate material. People brought in Tina Turner. The show is a folk musical. Bob Dylan is a folk singer. So you must bring in songs that were written by folk singers like Joni Mitchell. There's no showing off here, no riff fests. Bob Dylan doesn't show off. He's a poet.

He concludes, "The people who really impress me are people who are able to live in many worlds, those who live in a contemporary musical theater base, but are flexible, pliable, know how to sing in the style and the range required, have great musicality, and know how to communicate in whatever style is needed."

Choreographer/Director Andy Blankenbuehler on Embodying Culture

I met with Andy Blankenbuehler, who won the Tony Award and Drama Desk Award for choreographing *In the Heights,* a contemporary rock musical about three days in the lives of Dominican Americans residing in an inner-city neighborhood of New York City.[2] My intent was to talk to him specifically about what the body language needs to be at a contemporary pop audition. At the time we spoke, he was in the process of directing and choreographing *Bring It On,* a stage production based on a film in 2000 about rival squads of cheerleaders. Little did I know what I was in store for, as he shockingly admitted, "I don't consider myself to be a pop choreographer or a choreographer of contemporary musical theater. I'm a choreographer of musical theater. I would do anything to choreograph a musical set in the '40s.

Andy continues,

> I'm a conservative person from Cincinnati. I had to *learn* how to understand contemporary choreography to do *In the Heights.* If I want to move like someone on the street, I have to feel like somebody on the street. I have to know what the clothes feel like. I have to know what the shoes feel like. I have to know what the heat feels like. I had to learn. Once I have respect for those details, then I can put it in the dance step. I have to teach myself how to do it for every time period, because I have to be truthful. If you care about the details, it makes it better for everyone. It makes everything better. You do all that work, and there's so much more at stake. It is real, invested, and successful.

"Emotions are always relevant," he adds. "If the characters onstage are angst-ridden in 1940 or 2010, they still are both feeling angst. They just have different ways of dressing. Their angst still reaches its boiling point exactly the same way and for the same kind of reasons. The idea of going from anger to expressing yourself or feeling as if you'll bust has never changed. How you express anger has changed but the emotions are the same."

Asked how he puts facts drawn from his research into a performance, Andy comments, "For example, in the 1920s, the hemlines on skirts came up. The girls were footloose and fancy-free. They were living life because their ankles were showing. The Charleston was the music of the era, and they used the dance with its syncopation to express their newfound freedom. Someone could be walking down the street with that freedom, and it's the same as in the Heights when you're walking down the street after kissing a girl for the first time. There's a different beat, but the same freedom, the same musicality."

He concludes, "The core is truth, and, as an actor, you have to figure out the language. What you need is the intellect to connect, the emotion to understand, the technique to execute it. But all you have to do is figure it out. It's a math equation, applied to an important thing like, 'I need to boil water to cook food.' Understand what needs to be said, feel the authenticity of your connection to it. With that, anything is possible. Step into it. Try it on for size."

If Andy Blankenbuehler, a guy born and raised in Cincinnati, could study and master the intricate details of Dominican American culture in New York City, why couldn't you study and master the culture of any pop musical or rock musical that you have the chance to audition for? You can. You can figure out how to walk, talk, move, express yourself emotionally, and understand what your character's dreams, hopes, and aspirations are.

Welcome now to my anthropological dig through the pop culture of the 1950s to the present day. Let's begin at the beginning.

The Mid-'50s to the Mid-'60s

What was happening in pop culture during the earliest decade of rock and roll? There was now a TV set in every home. (What did we *do* before TV sets?! I guess we had to talk to each other.) Families gathered around the set to watch shows like *Leave It to Beaver, The Honeymooners, Ozzie and Harriet,* and *Howdy Doody,* as well as variety shows and dance programs like *American Bandstand* and *The Ed Sullivan Show.* Pop trends included hula-hoops, Barbie dolls, and drive-in movies. John F. Kennedy was elected, and then he was assassinated. Martin Luther King Jr. gave his unbelievable "I Have a Dream" speech. There was the passage of the Civil Rights Act.

Iconic figures of the era include Arthur Godfrey, Milton Berle, Sid Caesar, James Dean, Marilyn Monroe, Jack Kerouac and the Beat poets, the Smothers Brothers, the beautiful Shirley Chisholm, and Rosa Parks.

Iconic musicians and rock groups of the era include Little Richard, Fats Domino, Chuck Berry, Bill Haley and the Comets, Jerry

Lee Lewis, the Everly Brothers, Frankie Valli and the Four Seasons, Connie Francis, Buddy Holly, the Beach Boys, Fabian, Bobby Darin, and Elvis Presley (aka the King of Rock and Roll). Presley was the first white musician who truly celebrated how the African American community influenced him. His music successfully combines the pop and country music of his era, the gospel music he heard in church and at the all-night gospel sing-ins he frequently attended, and the rhythm and blues he absorbed on historic Beale Street in Memphis, Tennessee, as a teenager.[3]

"Beatlemania" was the term used for the mass hysteria that occurred when the Beatles led the British Invasion on American pop music and culture in 1963. Other great bands that followed in their footsteps by internationalizing the production of rock and roll were the Animals, Manfred Mann, Petula Clark, Herman's Hermits, and the Rolling Stones. But it was the Beatles who—after releasing their record during the time teenagers were on a break from school, performing on *The Ed Sullivan Show* in 1964, and admitting Elvis had a direct influence on their music—introduced us to the "rock group" based around guitar and drums.

Dusty Springfield, considered the finest white soul singer of the era, came from the British Invasion, but more importantly, she was the first public figure to create and host performances of her favorite little-known soul singers and top-selling Motown artists for British audiences in 1965. She styled her hair in a peroxide blonde beehive, wore evening gowns and a full face of make-up, and sang her heart on some of Burt Bacharach's greatest tunes. What a woman!

Motown came into vogue. Berry Gordy Jr. founded the Motown Label in Detroit in 1958 to sidestep the restrictions preventing African American performers from singing their own music on the radio or TV. Motown created careers for artists such as Stevie Wonder, Marvin Gaye, Smokey Robinson, Diana Ross and the Supremes, the Temptations, and the Jackson Five. By introducing black music into the mainstream music scene, Motown participated in the gradual breakdown of the racial barrier of segregation across the nation.

I'm glad you're reading this right now . . . it's what all the '50s and '60s rock musicals are about—and you *have* to factor it into your audition.

What were people like socially in the 1950s? Well, let's use *I Love Lucy* as an example of how they were was portrayed in the pop culture. Let's talk about the bedroom. Umm . . . couples slept in separate beds, you guys. Apparently people in the 1950s could get pregnant through "immaculate" conception! Lucille Ball was the first woman to show her pregnancy on national television, and guess what she had to call it? She had to say she was "expecting," as if she was waiting for a package in the mail.

Also, because there were no camera shots in the bathroom, you can assume that people didn't go pee-pee and poo-poo back then, either! The truth is that they did; they just didn't want anyone to know. They were being discreet, because there was no intimacy displayed in public at that time. If there was any sign of emotional "disturbance," the appropriate thing to do with a person of this nature was to give him or her electric shock treatments. Crazy, right?

Men and women had distinct and clear-cut gender roles. The men were the breadwinners. Women, if they were married, were housewives and stay-at-home mothers. If they were not, they were spinsters and were thought to be troubled and unmarriable.

People were polite, pristine, crisp, pressed, starched, appropriate, poised, and emotionally contained. They did not show their feelings. They presented a clean-cut and sophisticated facade. Even the "bad boys" of the 1950s were clean cut by today's standards. Rebels wore their greasy hair perfectly combed into a "DA." (DA stands for duck's ass, did you know that? This hairstyle mocked a duck's bottom—that is geeeeenius. That ass was in the back, with a pompadour quiff in the front.) People were big smokers. The bras women wore were cone-shaped so you couldn't see their natural curves. They also wore girdles to create a cleaner form and had their hair "done" (which means they had the crap teased out of their hair, which was then sprayed in place). Kids were taught to say, "Please" and "Thank you." They said, "Yes, sir" and "Yes, ma'am." Can you imagine? People were god-fearing, had tremendous pride in their country, and were very optimistic about life.

How should you dress for a 1950s or 1960s rock audition? To best capture the style of this era, your must think conservatively. Guys, wear an ironed, buttoned-down shirt and a clean pair of slacks. (I love that word "slacks"!) Ladies, be crisp. A simple fitted sweater or a buttoned-down shirt would look great on you, too. You can wear either a modest skirt or a pair of dark jeans tapered or rolled up at the ankles. A dress that is fitted is okay, but please keep your cleavage to yourself. And men and women took a lot of pride in their appearance, so for god's sake, comb your hair!

Think about the great rock musicals with which you are familiar that take place in this era. Wouldn't you agree that incorporating cool details like these into your audition could help you create an authentic performance that well represents this time period?

The Mid-'60s to the Mid-'70s

What was happening in popular culture from the late 1960s to the early 1970s? It was the era of the Vietnam War, the peace movement, racial tension, nonviolent social protest, the Black Power movement, the Woodstock Festival, be-ins, women's liberation, the founding of the National Organization for Women (NOW), *Sergeant Pepper's Lonely Hearts Club Band, Ms.* magazine, Marlo Thomas's *Free to Be You and Me,* the "Now Generation," communal living, the Fillmore Auditorium, Mod fashion, Jerry Rubin and Abbie Hoffman's Yippie movement, and draft dodging. People burned flags, bras, and draft cards. In 1973, the Supreme Court decided the *Roe v. Wade* case that struck down laws restricting abortion.

Iconic figures of the era include Timothy Leary, Gloria Steinem, Maharishi Mahesh Yogi, Twiggy, Andy Warhol, Peter Max, Malcolm X, Donny and Marie Osmond, Sonny and Cher, the Partridge Family, and Sid and Marty Krofft.

Iconic musicians and rock groups of the era include Jimi Hendrix; the Who; the Velvet Underground; Bob Dylan; Janis Joplin; the Doors; the Mamas and the Papas; Three Dog Night; Peter, Paul and Mary; Meatloaf; the Rolling Stones; and Simon and Garfunkel.

What were people like socially? People were losing everyone they cared about in such a violent way, for reasons entirely unnecessary, and for the first time in history they were watching it happen on television. The Vietnam War was traumatizing to the human spirit. The youth of the day could no longer suppress their feelings and act as if everything was okay, so they chose to break loose from conventional social mores and rebel. Many of them had no idea who they were or how they truly felt about anything. With the assistance of marijuana and psychedelic drugs, like LSD, they began altering their minds and expanding their souls. As a culture, Americans became mystical, spiritual, and began to soul search. They needed release, pleasure, contact, intimacy, expression, freedom, and change, inner peace, global peace, and absolute abandon. People went from sleeping in separate beds to sleeping with everyone they knew.

What should you wear to capture the hippie era? I went to pass out my business cards at the EPAs and ECCs for the revival of *Hair* and lost my mind when I saw girls wearing fake flowers in their hair and tie-dyed shirts that they'd bought the day before at TJ Maxx. The boys were just as unaware, because they were cleanly shaven. Remember, during that era, especially among members of the antiwar "counterculture," people lived in the park. They slept on the grass. They didn't shower. They didn't want to shave or cut their hair. That's why the show is called *Hair*.

So guys, grow out your facial hair for 1970s folk/rock auditions. This particular audition was posted on the Actors' Equity website a month before it took place. You would have known about it in plenty of time to get dirty-looking. *The clothes you wear need to feel like they are lived in,* like you've been wearing them day in and day out and sleeping in them, too! They must be so worn that they have taken your shape. And, for God's sake, *don't* comb your hair!

The Disco Era (Mid-'70s to Mid-'80s)

What was the most exciting thing happening in the popular culture of the late 1970s? Disco dancing. This is a prime example of how structure, needing to find its way back into people's lives, found its way in through the music of the day. In New York City, Studio 54 was the place to be. A world-famous discotheque located on West 54th street in Manhattan, it was a haven of drugs, celebrities, scandalous behavior, and sexual promiscuity. Even though excess was all around them, everybody was doing the hustle, a controlled partner dance form that combines tight footwork with smooth gestures.

The general public was now watching color TV—and right on time, too, because people of color were finally appearing on primetime television and in family hour sitcoms like *Chico and the Man, Good Times, The Jeffersons, Sanford and Son,* and *What's Happening!* During the day, kids got to watch afterschool specials, with *Schoolhouse Rock* and PSAs like *Time for Timer* and *The Bod Squad* as commercial breaks. At night, we also got *Soul Train, The Gong Show, Midnight Special*, and the debut of one of the greatest sketch comedy shows of all time, still on every weekend, *Saturday Night Live*.

Michael Jackson's album *Off the Wall* took over the Billboard music charts. People used 8-track tape players and welcomed their successor, cassette tapes. My favorite thing in the world to do as a kid in this era was to watch the Saturday night TV lineup of *Solid Gold* and *Dance Fever* followed by *The Love Boat* and *Fantasy Island.* One of my fondest memories was watching David Copperfield make Valerie Bertinelli disappear on national television while the Barry Manilow song "A Weekend in New England" was playing. I think this magic show took place on *Circus of the Stars.* Or maybe it was on *Battle of the Network Stars*. Look those shows up. They were brilliant!

In 1980, President Ronald Reagan took office. That spelled the beginning of the Reagan Era, the time in which the Wall Street boom made rich people richer and we saw the collapse of the Soviet Union, the tearing down of the Berlin Wall, and the end of the Cold War.

Iconic figures of the era include the Bionic Woman, Cher, Wonder Woman, Evil Knievel, Wolfman Jack, Casey Kasem (*American Top 40 Countdown* on radio), the Village People, Charlie's Angels, skater Dorothy Hamill, Doug Henning, the husband and wife mime team of Shields and Yarnell, Rip Taylor, and Foxy Brown. Notice that the iconic figures of the era changed from the previous decade's political figures into fantastic celebrity creatures.

Iconic musicians and musical groups of the era include Olivia Newton-John; Donna Summer; Earth, Wind and Fire; Michael Jackson; the Weather Girls; the Bee Gees; Kool and the Gang; Barry White; and Blondie. Did you know Blondie was the very first group to rap in a number-one hit song? Coincidentally, the song was called "Rapture."

What were people like socially? I like to call this decade the "Great Escape," as it involved unprecedented social transition and profound turbulence. It was an indulgent decade, decadent and sexy. Since many had decided to reject social restraints, pop culture asked them to leave their responsibilities behind. In music, the connection to rhythm was back (as opposed to the free-spirited style of the mid-'60s to mid-'70s), but now people disappeared into the music, into the high, into guilt-free sex, and into whatever felt good.

People became loose—too loose. They started getting themselves into big trouble by exhibiting incredible lust for pleasure and excess. Recreational drugs switched from marijuana and psychedelics to cocaine, as the cultural mood shifted from getting in touch with your feelings to staying up all night partying.

Look at John Travolta (Tony) and Karen Lynn Gorney (Stephanie) in the 1977 movie *Saturday Night Fever*. When on the dance floor, their moves were choreographed to be profoundly crisp and clean. However, inside of that "crispness," their moves are fluid, loose, languid, relaxed, and easy. Their clothes are tailored and really tight, but take a look at their legs! You'll see the men (and women) are wearing bell-bottom pantsuits! With platform shoes! This was truly an era of freedom inside a structure.

What should you wear to your disco-era auditions? I wished so badly that I wasn't a kid in the disco era. You know I'd have been shaking my booty in the finest polyester leisure suit. Since that outfit would feel like a bit much for an audition, however, your best bet, if you're a woman, is to wear a long and flowing dress that is form-fitting in the top. Men, if you've got a soft shirt and pants tight in the crotch with bell-bottoms, go for it. But remember that your colors must not be *loud.* Let your acting do the talking, not your shirt!

After the country went from holding to not-withholding, whatever structure there was wasn't enough—because that freedom came with a price. By the early 1980s, the AIDS epidemic ended the sexual revolution that started in the 1960s. People were losing friends they loved, and they felt out of control because the Great Escape had taken them too far outside of themselves. They were desperate to be present with their emotions again, but they didn't know how. All they knew was that they needed to come back from the edge. They needed to sober up. As a result, folks decided to find a new way to express who they were and how they felt.

The Rest of the '80s

Ahhh, the '80s! What a colorful and often embarrassing time of many of our lives. If you are reading this and you were around in the '80s, you know exactly what I'm talking about. If you weren't, check out the facts about the decade and watch some old music videos on YouTube. You won't believe your eyes. Better yet, you'll be blinded by neon—or "Blinded by Science."

What were the amazing things happening in popular culture during the mid- to late 1980s? First and foremost, MTV launched in 1981 and became the first TV station whose sole purpose was to play rock videos. As such, it directly influenced the music industry and pop culture. "Video Killed the Radio Star" by the Buggles was the first video ever played on MTV. VH1 surfaced in 1985. The movies *Flashdance, Fame, The Breakfast Club, Pretty in Pink,* and *St. Elmo's Fire* gave voice to a new generation. *Miami Vice, Who's the Boss, Gimme a Break, Square Pegs,* and *Charles in Charge* were some of the silly, incredibly popular shows on television. I had the biggest—and I am not kidding when I say the BIGGEST—crush on Molly Ringwald. My crush was so big that my gym teacher cut out a picture of her and said, "Here, I brought you a picture of your girlfriend for your scrapbook." How did she know I had a scrapbook? Girlfriend? Oopsie!

People played with Rubik's Cubes, kept their schoolwork in their Trapper Keepers, and the cool place to be was at the arcade, playing Pac-Man, Ms. Pac-Man, Tron, Galaga, Dig Dug, and Donkey Kong. Atari and ColecoVision were examples of early home video game systems.

Powerful things were going on in the music industry, stemming from people's desire to now take on world issues. In 1985, Bob Geldof created both Band-Aid (a group of British and Irish artists who put together "Do They Know It's Christmas?") and Live Aid (twin rock concerts, held in London and Philadelphia on the same day, with artists from around the world) to raise money and awareness for famine relief in Ethiopia. The same year, Michael Jackson and Lionel Ritchie wrote the song "We Are the World." A group of American vocalists sang on the incredible album made of that song, which was produced as a fundraiser by USA for Africa. In 1986, a charity "single" was similarly recorded that raised three million dollars for the American Foundation for AIDS research: Burt Bacharach and Carole Bayer Sager's "That's What Friends Are For." These three acts of political and social activism helped open people's eyes to what was going on outside of their comfort zone and encouraged generosity.

Iconic figures of the era include Michael Jackson, Quincy Jones, Indira Gandhi, Jane Fonda (with her workout videos), Mr. T, Pee-Wee Herman, Eddie Murphy, the California Raisins, Spuds MacKenzie, the Coreys (Corey Feldman and the late Corey Haim), Kirk Cameron, and Max Headroom.

Iconic musicians of the era include Prince, Janet Jackson, Whitney Houston, Cyndi Lauper, Madonna, Taylor Dayne, Flock of Seagulls, Boy George, Duran Duran, the Cure, Twisted Sister, Def Leppard, Cinderella, Poison, Mötley Crüe, and Van Halen. Less colorful, but certainly musically dramatic, were Journey, Foreigner, George Michael, Rick Springfield, U2, INXS, the Police, Peter Gabriel, Billy Joel, Pat Benatar, Scandal, Men at Work, Heart, and Bon Jovi.

What were these crazy people like? They were outrageous, loud, and playful. You see, the AIDS epidemic devastated many lives just as the Vietnam War had done a generation earlier, so it had a tremendous influence on the popular music, which began expressing itself in a way it never had. People took themselves and the fun they needed to have very seriously. The music had to lighten up. As we were now exposed to programmed music, our songs became fun, light, easy, buoyant, and distracting entertainment, as if musicians were reintroducing the lightness of the 1950s. As a direct influence of the 1983 movie *Valley Girl,* kids began using expressions like "Omigod," "Like, totally," "Barf me out," "Gag me with a spoon," and "tubular."

Let's be frank. Many of the '80s artists, in both pop *and rock*, took their inspiration directly from David Bowie and the character Ziggy Stardust that he created in the 1970s. Ziggy was androgynous. He wore a full face of makeup; clothes so tight you could see his business; had spiky, angular hair; and was dramatic and colorful. Bowie clearly influenced '80s rock groups like Cinderella and Poison. But just look at electronic pop culture musicians such as Duran Duran, Cyndi Lauper, Boy George, a-ha, and Kajagoogoo. Can you see his influence on them too?

The way people were behaving, dressing, and expressing themselves in the '80s would be construed as really silly by today's standards. This is marvelous when you are auditioning for '80s rock musicals, like *The Wedding Singer,* because in order to tip your hat to the style, you have to accentuate the colorfulness of the era and its drama to the point of making fun of it. It's almost a lampooning of oneself. You literally have to take yourself so seriously that it becomes hysterical to any onlooker.

What's the fashion sense of the '80s'? If you're going to audition for an extreme '80s musical, like *Rock of Ages* or *The Wedding Singer,* crimping your hair and wearing acid-washed jeans wouldn't hurt you one bit. But if your audition is for any musical that was written *about* that era, like *Fame* or *Footloose,* which wouldn't lampoon the '80s, I'd just wear a clean pair of jeans and a nice shirt, and women, little heels would be perfect. My suggestion is to simply look cool! No matter what, this is a rock musical.

The '90s to Now

After making spectacles of themselves in the '80s, in the '90s people felt the need to rein it in, and boy did they ever! Let me preface this section by saying that a lot has gone on in the last twenty years in the music scene. While I don't believe the 1990s and 2000s should necessarily be coupled together because popular music has kept changing during this time, right now it's the easiest way to define the sound that musical theater producers and directors are looking to hear in auditions for their contemporary shows. Therefore, you will simply find twenty years' worth of clues here on what has influenced this kind of music. What is essential for you to understand is that there is a dark side and a light side to the music of the period.

During the last two decades, people have developed an insatiable need for instant gratification. The Internet, laptops, cybersex, cell phones, Blackberries, Friendster, iPods, MySpace, Facebook, Twitter, gastric bypass surgery, reconstructive surgery, liposuction, Botox, breast implants, cloning, and so on are indicative of this need for speed. Technology has brought people good things, like stem cell research, electrocardiograms, and solar power panels—as well as other tools of sustainable design that are enabling us to "go green." Ground was broken in filmmaking, with the birth of Pixar; computerized special effects shown in the Harry Potter film series, *The Lord of the Rings, The X-Men,* and *Avatar;* and the regeneration of 3-D movies—created digitally.

Pop culture and musical theater are now officially overlapping. I chatted with my friend Mark Blankenship, a critic and journalist who's written about theatre for *The New York Times* and *Variety* and who's covered pop culture for NPR, *The Joy Behar Show,* and his own website, The Critical Condition (thecriticalcondition.com). This is what we found:

Between 2000 and 2010, musical theater became more integral to pop culture than it had been since the '60s (with *Fiddler on the Roof* and *West Side Story* as our movie musicals). Today, the movies have had *Chicago, Hairspray,* and *Dreamgirls.* Television had *High School Musical,* and Broadway night on *American Idol.*

A slew of British and American reality shows—including *Legally Blonde, The Musical: The Search for Elle Woods; Grease: You're the One That I Want;* and *How Do You Solve a Problem Like a Maria?;* and *Any Dream Will Do*—had unknowns competing by singing pop songs as well as show tunes. Nothing blurs the line between legit music and pop music like two wannabe "Nancies" competing to be in *Oliver,* wearing hot pink corsets and bloomers and singing "The Rose," by Bette Midler.

But these examples are just the opening act for the phenomenon *Glee,* the Fox television series about a high school glee club. The show is essentially a jukebox musical: It anchors every episode with cast performances of pop songs and show tunes, and it stars Broadway vets like Matthew Morrison and Lea Michele. As of this writing, it has sent eight albums into the U.S. top ten and charted almost 100 hit singles, including covers of show tunes like "Defying Gravity," "Maybe This Time," "Don't Rain on My Parade," and even "Le Jazz Hot" from *Victor/Victoria.* You can't get through an episode without being immersed in some aspect of musical theater.

In other words, *Glee* epitomizes the forces that have pushed musical theater back into the mainstream of pop culture.

Granted, this trend has drawbacks. Just ask anyone who has seen an *American Idol* alum give a half-baked Broadway performance. But overall, when musicals become pop culture, millions of people gain the tools to understand and love what theater can do. And that opens new doors for musical theater artists.

We can also be very thankful for the new trend that's happening as we speak, where there are several made for TV musicals that are being birthed by the musical theatre community. Take for example, the TV series *Smash* which is being written by playwright Teresa Rebeck with songs by the team of Mark Shaiman and Scott Whittman, and directed by Michael Mayer for NBC. It's about the process of conceiving, creating, rehearsing, and producing a fictional musical. This was Steven Speilberg's brainchild. I am so excited to watch the whole world get fall in love with our community, and how we tell our stories.

Some of the tragic events that went on during these two decades are the 1999 Columbine High School shooting; the September 11, 2001, terrorist attacks on the World Trade Center in New York and the Pentagon in Washington, DC; and wars in Iraq and Afghanistan. In 2007, there was a meltdown on Wall Street and a corruption scandal that began a worldwide recession in which millions of people lost their savings, houses, and jobs. There was also the horrific manmade disaster of the BP Horizon Oil rig explosion, which poured crude oil into the Gulf of Mexico for months.

In my opinion, Mother Nature is so tired of how we treat each other, and ourselves, and the earth, that she has created some of the worst natural disasters we've had to date. Washed over with emotion, she caused the tsunami in Thailand; spinning with fury, she ruined lives through Hurricane Katrina; and shaken to the core with anger, she gave Haiti an earthquake it may never recover from.

In maintaining the delicate balance of the universe, in these decades there has been progress in the struggle to legalize civil unions and recognize marriages between gay couples. In 2007, we witnessed a presidential debate between a white woman and a black man. President Barack H. Obama won the election and became the 44th leader of the United States. Moments like his inauguration, which symbolize hope and possibility, and demonstrate progress for formerly oppressed and disenfranchised people, gave many of us tremendous faith that ultimately we're going to be okay.

There were two scenes in music during this era: the rock scene and the pop scene. Let's begin by looking at contemporary rock as it relates to musical theater. The rock scene, in its extreme, takes us to the dark side of the emotional spectrum.

The Contemporary Rock Scene

Through the movies and television of the 1990s, we were introduced to a stereotypical new form of young American known as the "slacker" and to the new musical archetype of grunge rock. We saw slackers and grunge rock in movies like *Heathers, Clerks, Reality Bites,* and *High Fidelity*. Television shows like *My So-Called Life* and *Dawson's Creek* with emotionally ambivalent lead characters also exposed teenage viewers to musical trends and emerging bands. The cartoon *Daria,* named for its central character, a bored slacker-type college student, ran on MTV. On our home computers and Playstations, we played games like Grand Theft Auto and, more recently, Guitar Hero.

The humor of the 1990s till now can be base and celebrate the cynicism of the slacking lifestyle. Think about comedians Chris Farley, David Spade, Adam Sandler, and Will Ferrell; the movies *Old School* and *Napoleon Dynamite*; and the cartoons created as much for grownups as for kids: *Beavis and Butthead, Ren and Stimpy, South Park, The Simpsons, King of the Hill,* and *Family Guy.* These demonstrate the dark humor of our current generation.

Iconic figures of this era include Roseanne, Rosie O'Donnell, Jerry Seinfeld, Oprah, Matt Damon and Ben Affleck, Al Gore, Dr. Phil, Tom Cruise (and Scientology), the late Heath Ledger, Courtney Love, Ellen De Generes, the late Michael Jackson, the ladies of the TV show *The View,* Sonia Sotomayor, Tiger Woods, Martha Stewart, Eminem, and Angelina Jolie.

Iconic musicians of this era include Eddie Vedder and Pearl Jam, Alanis Morissette, REM, Annie Lennox, Sinead O'Connor, the Red Hot Chili Peppers, Tori Amos, 4 Non Blondes, Nine Inch Nails, Oasis, No Doubt, Green Day, Maroon 5, Pink, Avril Lavigne, Soundgarden, and the Goo Goo Dolls. Let's not forget the extraordinary movement in women's music that started with Lilith Fair, created by Sarah McLachlan.

In addition to grunge, alt rock, and indie rock, we were introduced to emo music (which is shorthand for emotional music). Rites of Spring was the first emo band to break away from the rebellious punk sound in their choice of guitar melodies, confessional lyrics, and the personal storytelling that came from the punk rock scene in the '80s. From the '80s to now, bands like Siouxsie and the Banshees, the Cure, the Smiths, Jawbreaker, Mineral, Sunny Day Real Estate, the Pixies, Garbage, Sonic Youth, Paramore, Fall Out Boy, Weezer, Dashboard Confessional, My Chemical Romance, Panic at the Disco, and Death Cab for Cutie master what I'd call a "folk take" on punk music.

What were people like socially in the 1990s and 2000s? Well, I'd say the essence of this time period, in one word, was angst. The music, the lyrics, the feeling of the era were like a great ache. We covered ourselves in tattoos and piercings, and wore combat boots and flannel. We went from "This is me. This is who I am. This is how I feel," to "You don't understand me. You'll never understand me. I am alone in this feeling and alone in the world." Our youth felt tortured and tormented, and their parents went into a state of panic and terror at the darkness they were feeling, screaming "Help! My son is dressed in black and hiding in his room with the lights out!"

Oprah Winfrey was there with her afternoon talk show, ready and able to talk about everything, and then in came Dr. Phil, self-help books, the diagnosis of ADHD, and the over-prescribing of drugs like Ritalin for kids and Lexapro and Prozac for adults. The sentiment of adults toward children was, "I can't handle your pain. Let's fix it. Let's make it go away." But some of our greatest young rock performers insisted on being heard and having their pain regardless of how much it hurt them, or anyone else.

When you audition for a contemporary rock musical—one either written in this era or set in this era—you need to achieve a sentiment that represents the voice of the underdog, the dark soul, the misguided. We have the late, great Kurt Cobain, the brilliant leader of Nirvana (whose pain led him to die of a heroin overdose), to thank for creating that opportunity for us.

What would be an appropriate way for you to dress for a rock musical audition? The days of wrap dresses and character shoes are over, so wear whatever makes you feel comfortable. Make sure it is clean and in good condition, but be casual, be real, be you. Rock musicals on the whole are relaxed, so it's best to dress that way and be authentic.

The Contemporary Pop Scene

Pop music icons and social trends of the last two decades are a bit different from the rock music icons and trends we've just seen. Obviously, historical events were similar; however, on the pop side of things—the lighter side of life—many Americans became obsessed with the cult of celebrity. Finding life tough, people wanted to be diverted. Instead of wanting to express their pain, they loved to intrude voyeuristically upon the private lives of the rich, famous, and stupid, and observe their pain. People loved watching good-looking socialites create scandals outside nightclubs with their narcissistic behavior. And if young movie stars wanted to take drugs, blow their millions, and piss their careers down the toilet, why not watch it for the sake of amusement? The hyper-attention to minuscule details of celebrities' lives in magazines, on TV, and via the Internet evolved into an epoch of reality television programming, where literally anyone could be famous if he or she did something extreme enough— and almost everyone wanted to be famous. And YouTube was there.

Iconic pop culture figures of the era of the '90s to the '00s include the casts of *90210* and *Friends,* Paris Hilton, Perez Hilton, Tyra Banks, Mary-Kate and Ashley Olsen, Simon Cowell, Donald Trump, Britney Spears, Lindsay Lohan, P. Diddy, Kanye West, Justin Beiber, and, of course, Lady Gaga.

Iconic pop musicians of the era include Dee Lite, Backstreet Boys, Mariah Carey, Jennifer Lopez, N*Sync, Spice Girls, Boyz

II Men, Madonna (and her album *Vogue*), Justin Timberlake, Destiny's Child, Britney Spears, Jessica Simpson, Will Smith, Vanilla Ice, Lauryn Hill, Christina Aguilera, Rihanna, Jay-Z, Tupac Shakur, Missy Elliott, Alicia Keys, Black Eyed Peas, Pink, and Katy Perry. The pop music of this generation includes overproduced, super-sexualized, provocative, and dynamic hyper-vocalizations. This style of music production had its origins in the soulfulness of R&B and hip-hop. Rap gave urban youth without resources like money or training an opportunity to express themselves and the way they understood life in their own language.

Popular trends of the era include an assortment of reality television shows, which include competitions and project shows like *Project Runway, America's Next Top Model, RuPaul's Drag Race, The Apprentice, Survivor, The Biggest Loser, Dancing with the Stars, Top Chef, So You Think You Can Dance? Extreme Makeover,* and, of course, *American Idol,* as well as voyeuristic programs like *The Real World, The Real Housewives of Orange County, Rock of Love, The Hills, Jersey Shore,* and *Celebrity Rehab.*

How should you dress for a pop musical audition? Let's face it, pop style is sexy. So be your sexy self. A tight pair of jeans and a sexy tee-shirt, with heels or Converse sneakers is a cool look for the girls. The choice of heels versus sneakers depends on whether or not you are going to audition for a sexpot. Guys, wear something that's comfy, cool, relaxed, and clean. Being sexy does not mean being trashy. Whereas you should dress for a contemporary rock audition as if you are selecting the clothes you would wear to hang out with your friends, for a pop audition you would ask yourself, "What would I wear if I was going on a date?"

What to Do with This Information

There were hundreds of other singers and bands, many more great leaders, and numerous other important, life-altering events happening in the world during the time periods we've discussed here. Use the preceding lists of information to get a sense of the essence of what these eras felt like to the people who lived in them. Then go out and do more research on your own. These references are here to help you evoke the time period, not for you to use as research to write a doctoral thesis.

I must end this chapter with an essential message. In this chapter, I discussed what each generation went through in order for music to evolve in the way that it has. Thus, I believe it is imperative to have an element of gratitude inside of you when you present any song. I honor, respect, and thank any artist, politician, or revolutionary who changed the face of music, and art, theater, and humanity. This means to sing a Motown song, you must honor the African American community and what they went through to create the brilliant R&B music that you now get to sing. The depth of emotion felt from the loss of loved ones in the Vietnam War must be a part of the essence of what you sing in a '70s musical—even if your song is lighthearted. Use the lightheartedness to lift the darkness. Similarly, disco music and its progression into '80s pop afforded us an escape from thinking about all the friends we were losing to AIDS. The best way to show gratitude is by loving the song you sing and understanding its purpose in music and society.

Please don't ever leave out the element of the weight that each given generation had to carry in order to choose to express themselves in the way they sang. That weight adds the texture, depth, color, and life to your auditions that these songs so richly deserve.

Also, let your gratitude to the artist who gave you a song with which to connect become part of your performance as well. For example, if you are white, and you are singing a song that was written (and/or performed) by a black person, can you perform this tune in a way that you are saying, "I love the person who wrote this song. I don't care if he's black. He's my friend. And I am going to honor and celebrate him and who he is when I sing this song, not take it from him and sterilize it"? Can you sing this song with the purpose of personally contributing to the end of segregation? Because we aren't "black and white," we are all beautiful shades of brown. If you do, the casting director, the director, the music director, the writer, and anyone else will think, "Holy shit! This actor really did their homework. They understand what time period the show is set in and took the time to care what that meant. This actor will care about the integrity of our production."

Isn't the idea of doing an audition more thrilling once you understand that putting historical detail and the essence of the human concerns that your character would have had into your work can help you win over the creative team? In the next chapter, we're going to look at how to pick a song that captures the essence of the era in which the play you're auditioning for takes place so you can express it.

3

Picking a Rock Song

How do I pick a rock song? I don't listen to the radio. I grew up singing show tunes!" That's what I hear every time someone steps foot in my office for the first time.

Guess what? Looking for music can be an absolute *blast* once you figure out how to do it. But before we get into discussing *anything* about the type of songs you need to pick, you first have to be clear on what rock musicals *are*. When you've got a grasp on this, you can go on to identify the essence of the rock musicals that are being produced. That makes picking a bunch of really hot rock songs perfectly suited for your auditions *super easy*.

What Is a Rock Musical?

I can't tell you how many people are confused about which shows on Broadway are actually rock musicals. They ask, "Is *Jersey Boys* a rock musical? And what about *Billy Elliot*?"

For the love of God, *yes!*

The term "rock musical" is a sweeping generalization applied to musicals that cannot be considered classical or legit. But in fact, productions in the rock category include all of the following types of music:

- ► 1950s and 1960s Motown and rock and roll
- ► 1970s rock/folk
- ► Mid-1970s to mid-'80s disco
- ► 1980s pop and rock
- ► Contemporary rock (1990s to the present)
- ► Contemporary pop (1990s to the present)
- ► Blues
- ► Country
- ► Gospel
- ► Rhythm and blues (R&B)
- ► Folk

A Brief Chronology of Pop/Rock Musicals

Take a peek at this chronological list of rock musicals drawn from the Broadway and Off-Broadway scenes since *Bye Bye Birdie* opened in 1960. Notice the asterisk placed next to certain shows. That asterisk indicates that although a show was written in one era, its story takes place in another. The important thing for you to know about a show when you are picking a song to audition with is the *era in which the story takes place.*

Bye Bye Birdie (1960)
Hair (1968)
Promises, Promises (1968)
The Me Nobody Knows (1970)
Jesus Christ Superstar (1971)
Godspell (1971)
Grease (1972)*
The Wiz (1975)
The Rocky Horror Show (1975)
Dreamgirls (1981)*
Starlight Express (1984)
Song and Dance (1985)
Chess (1988)
Starmites (1989)
Tommy (1992)*
Rent (1996)
Zombie Prom (1996)*
The Lion King (1997)
Hedwig and the Angry Inch (1998)
Fame (1998)*
Footloose (1999)*
Saturday Night Fever (1999)*
The Civil War (1999)
Aida (2000)
The Full Monty (2000)
Mamma Mia! (2000)
Bat Boy (2001)
We Will Rock You (2002)
Hairspray (2002)*
Zanna, Don't! (2002)
Taboo (2002)*
Bare (2004)
Altar Boyz (2005)
All Shook Up (2005)*
The Color Purple (2005)*
Jersey Boys (2006)*
The Wedding Singer (2006)*
Legally Blonde (2007)
Spring Awakening (2007)
Xanadu (2007)*
Shrek (2008)
Billy Elliot (2008)

Passing Strange (2008)
Rock of Ages (2009)*
Memphis (2009)*
Next to Normal (2009)
American Idiot (2010)
Bloody Bloody Andrew Jackson (2010)
Women on the Verge of a Nervous Breakdown (2010)
Spiderman (2010)
Bring It On (2011)
Priscilla (2011)

That's a lot of rock musicals. If you were to audition for any of these shows today, not only would you *have* to sing a rock song, you would need about four or five *different* songs to cover their different styles!

The First Step in Picking the Right Song for an Audition

To find great songs for your audition book, I want you to first take a look at the *casting breakdowns*. Before holding auditions, the casting office, along with the creative team, sends out details about the show and roles that have not yet been cast so that talent agents can submit their clients for these roles. These breakdowns are also posted on the Actors' Equity website (ActorsEquity.org) and on Backstage.com, which is open to folks who don't have theatrical representation...yet.

Most important is that breakdowns also suggest the type of song that the casting team would like to hear actors sing. A breakdown for *Hair,* for example, might read: "Bring in a 1970s rock song." A breakdown for *Rock of Ages* might read, "Bring in a 1980s rock ballad." Even though they are simple, such instructions are valuable in pointing you in the right direction.

Casting directors sometimes won't refer to an era at all in the breakdown. They'll just say, "Bring in a pop/rock song." In cases like this, it's up to *you* to research the show and figure out what *kind* of pop/rock musical it is. You have to do your best to get your hands on the specifics you need because creative teams have a tendency to generalize.

To be fair, they are busy. They don't have time to talk you through all the details. They're putting on a show!

Is It Pop or Rock?

When casting directors ask you for a "pop/rock" song, don't you find that confusing? Pop and rock are very different from each other; although, in truth, many of your favorite tunes are likely to fall into both categories. Want to know the difference?

Pop: Pop means popular culture. This type of song has a catchy melody and satisfies many different music appetites. When it is written, the songwriter intends for it to become a hit on the radio so people will want to buy the album or track. Such a song usually has danceable beats that make it irresistible. That's the source of its mass appeal.

Rock: Rock musicians are less interested in creating "hits" and more interested in creating songs that are authentic expressions of their emotions and their musicianship. The authenticity of the sound is based in electric guitar, a heavy bass sound, and drums. Rock is divided into subcultures like classic, indie (meaning the band is self-producing or "independent" of a record label), alternative, and punk.

Once you have identified the era in which the story takes place, you then need to determine if the music in the score is pop or rock.

Finding Great Songs That Fit the Genre and Era

When you understand the era and you know the difference between pop and rock, the next step will be to look at all the great singers whose songs would be perfect to audition with. For the most part, popular songs from mainstream singers in a given era will fit a show written about that era. For example, Janis Joplin, who sang in the late 1960s, wrote songs that are perfect for auditions for *Hair.* Whitney Houston's up-tempo numbers from the 1980s are suitable when auditioning for *Mamma Mia.* The tunes of Fall Out Boy, an emo-rock band from the mid-2000s, are great to sing if you're trying to get a role in *Bloody Bloody Andrew Jackson* or *American Idiot.*

Just like some shows are written in one era but capture the feel of another, there are also songs written in one era that capture the feel of another.

The Feel of It

I sat in on the EPAs for the musical *Memphis.* Although the breakdown said only that the casting directors wanted actors to prepare "a pop/rock song," for *Memphis* auditions they specifically needed to hear blues, Motown, and rock and roll from the '50s. You see, the show, which won four Tony Awards in 2010, including Best Musical, "is about a white radio DJ who wants to change the world and a black club singer who is ready for her big break."[1] You want to know something really cool? The score was written by David Bryan, the keyboardist from the band Bon Jovi—a contemporary rock musician.

So many different kinds of songs worked in the auditions. I heard people audition with tunes from the 1950s popularized by Otis Redding, Aretha Franklin, Martha and the Vandellas, Jackie Wilson, Sam Cooke, and Stevie Wonder. But I also heard successful auditions from actors singing the songs of Fats Waller, a jazz legend in the '20s and '30s, and Whitney Houston, the queen of '80s pop . . . Those two eras are entirely different than the era in which *Memphis* is set. But their music fit the production like a glove because the songs of Waller and Houston could be *performed* like '50s or '60s tunes.

We heard one actor treat a Bon Jovi song like an old blues ballad. Another actor brought in "Gimme the Ball," a legit tune from the Broadway musical *A Chorus Line*. His audition was successful because he treated it like a '50s Motown tune. Then an actor brought in the pop song "Hey Ya" from the hip-hop group Outkast. His performance was amazing! If you've ever watched the Outkast video of "Hey Ya," it looks as if they are a '50s band making a guest appearance on a TV variety show like *The Corny Collins Show* in *Hairspray*. He was clearly inspired by the video. All these brilliant and intuitive performers chose these songs and handled their performances like they were people living in the '50s. As a result, their headshots and résumés got put in the casting directors' "yes" pile. By the way, there are actually *two* yes piles. If a performer is amazing, but not right for the show, they got put into the second yes pile, which is the "yes, you're *great* and I want to see you for a different project" pile.

What didn't work that day at the auditions was when I could tell that actors had seen the instruction "bring in a pop/rock song" on the breakdown, and didn't think to ask, "What era does the show take place in?" Consequently they gave a contemporary pop/rock performance as opposed to one inspired by the '50s. It happened a lot that day. In the end, the "no" pile was much bigger than the "yes" pile because of it.

What I am saying here, my child, is that songs don't have to be from the same era in which the show was written, however they do need to be performed *as if they were.*

What your audition song needs to do is to capture the *essence* of the show. What do I mean by the word "essence"? The way something feels. Get used to this word. I'm going to use it a lot. The music and sentiment of your song need to *feel* like the show. Your performance also needs to *feel* like the show.

There are so many wonderful places to look for music. Places you would never ever think to look.

All right. *The next few sections of this chapter are going to rock your world.* We are going to take a quick look at the eras in which all sorts of beautiful shows deliciously fall, and where to find songs that would be great specifically when auditioning for these shows. To the creative teams of any shows I do not mention, I really want to say thank you. Your contribution to the theater world is awesome. Please do not let this be a reflection of your success.

Rock Music of the 1950s and 1960s

The breakdown for an audition for one of the following shows *should* say: "Bring in a '50s or '60s pop or rock song." This genre of rock musical requires you to sing a Motown or rock and roll song, as it dramatically covers the mid-'50s to the mid-'60s.

All Shook Up
Baby It's You!
Beehive
The Buddy Holly Story
Cry Baby
Dreamgirls
Forever Plaid
Grease
Hairspray
Jersey Boys
Leader of the Pack
Little Shop of Horrors
The Marvelous Wonderettes
Memphis
Million Dollar Quartet
Promises, Promises
Shout
Smokey Joe's Café

When I was telling a class that *The Little Shop of Horrors* was a '50s musical, a female student challenged me, "Yeah, but Sheri, the show was produced Off-Broadway in 1982 and Audrey's music is composed by Alan Menken, which means it is much more 'musical-theater-y' than typical early '60s rock."

My response to that was, "Yes, darling. But in its essence the entire piece is a doo wop musical; therefore you need to find a great girl's song off the radio from the doo wop or early Motown era that has a great storyline so that you can create a character like Audrey for your audition."

Make sense? Again, *your song needs to capture the essence of the show.* Although Alan Menken is a contemporary pop musical theater writer and Marc Shaiman, the composer of *Hairspray* and *Catch Me If You Can,* is a contemporary pop composer, lyricist, and arranger (he was Bette Midler's musical director for several projects), both men wrote shows that were reminiscent of the late '50s to the early '60s.

There are tons of great places to look for music that covers this era, which boasts a diverse palette of rock and roll, Motown, rhythm and blues, and doo wop. To me, a phenomenal place to look for flawless audition songs is within the song lists of the best-loved songwriters of this particular time period.

Along with the brilliance of Burt Bacharach and the other Brill Building artists I mentioned in Chapter 1, don't forget to look up the writing team of Holland-Dozier-Holland, made up of Lamont Dozier and the brothers Brian Holland and Eddie Holland Jr., as these guys were major hitmakers in the 1960s. Together they composed over 200 songs, including some of the biggest soul hits ever written, songs like "Baby Love," "Stop in the Name of Love," "Nowhere to Run," and "Where Did Our Love Go?"

Many contemporary pop writers from the last thirty years absolutely love the sound of the '50s and '60s. You can hear the influence of these decades in their songs. These artists are also fantastic resources for songs that communicate the essence of this era. To find audition pieces, you need to look up the work of these artists.

Billy Joel
The Go-Go's
The B-52's
The Stray Cats
Adam Ant
Jeff Beck (*Rock 'n' Roll Party Honoring Les Paul*)
Huey Lewis and the News
Amy Winehouse (a hot sloppy mess in her personal life, her album *Back to Black* is absolute Motown perfection)
Bruno Mars
John Legend
Prince (old James Brown kinda soul)

Any of these songwriters will guarantee that you will find an unbelievable audition song for a 1950s or 1960s rock musical in their body of work.

Rock Music of the 1970s

The breakdown for an audition for one of the following shows *should* say: "Bring in a '70s rock or folk song." Your song selection therefore should be a tune written anytime between 1965 and 1975, give or take a year here and there.

> *Godspell*
> *Hair*
> *Hedwig and the Angry Inch*
> *Jesus Christ Superstar*
> *The Me Nobody Knows*
> *The Rocky Horror Show*
> *Tommy*
> *Two Gentlemen of Verona*
> *We Will Rock You*

For the Broadway revival of *Godspell*, casting directors from Telsey and Company were asking for either a pop song or a contemporary musical theater song in the style of Stephen Schwartz. Given this instruction, this is where you would intuit that the pop sound the producers want to hear doesn't come from an artist like Christina Aguilera, Whitney Houston, or Justin Timberlake. If you look at Schwartz' show *Pippin*, you'll find "Corner of the Sky," a perfect representation of both the feel of the '70s and of Schwartz's musical style. This era asks for the raw, poetic nature of an authentic 1970s rock tune. The songs of so } many great artists, especially those whose music is timeless, would be perfect.

What do I mean when I call an artist "timeless"? These geniuses have created literally *decades* of brilliant music that could be sung for auditions in many different eras and genres. You could sing an Aretha Franklin song for shows set in the '50s, '60s, and '70s, in the style of blues, or R&B, or contemporary rock. You can sing her music for just about anything because her canon spans so many decades and styles. It is also because the honesty with which she communicates her music doesn't have era-specific musical references in it. This principle holds true for all timeless artists. Artists in this category include:

> Stevie Wonder
> Aretha Franklin
> Michael Jackson
> Elton John (collaborating with lyricist Bernie Taupin)
> Joe Cocker
> Tina Turner
> Aerosmith
> The Beatles
> Heart

Would you like to look up a *really* great songwriter from this era? She's a songwriter you need to know about because she is one of the greatest that has ever lived. Although she didn't necessarily write *for* other singers, her music is so dynamic and extraordinary that it was recorded during this era by Barbra Streisand; Three Dog Night; the Fifth Dimension; Blood, Sweat and Tears; Linda Ronstadt; Peter, Paul and Mary; and Thelma Houston. You can hear her influence when listening to singers who loved her, stars like Elton John, Joni Mitchell, Kate Bush, Elvis Costello, Rickie Lee Jones, and Carole King (herself one of the greatest songwriters of all time). Their music was directly inspired by her ability to fuse doo wop, rock, soul, jazz, folk, and blues. They'll tell you so.

Her name is Laura Nyro.

You may find the depth of Nyro's influence on our musical theater writers intriguing. In a biography of Nyro, *Soul Picnic* by Michele Kort, a photograph is printed showing Nyro and Stephen Sondheim hanging out together in Sondheim's apartment listening to music. He was such a fan of Nyro's song "Stoned Soul Picnic" that, according to Kort, "Sondheim said that, in its complexity, economy, and spontaneity, it summed up for him what music was all about."[2] And if you look carefully at the vocal selections of the musical *Godspell,* in the upper left-hand corner of the sheet music for "O Bless the Lord," the suggestion for how to style this gorgeous song is "à la Laura Nyro." She will change your life, I promise you.

Disco Music of the Mid-'70s to the Mid-'80s

The breakdown for an audition for one of the following shows would say: "Bring in a disco song."

> *Mamma Mia!*
> *Priscilla, Queen of the Desert*
> *Saturday Night Fever*
> *Sister Act*
> *The Wiz*
> *Xanadu*

There is no mistaking a disco tune from any other. A disco tune will evoke what all these shows are looking for, energy that makes your audience want to get up and boogie down! Olivia Newton-John was a big influence on the disco era, starring in the 1980 film *Xanadu* (which took place at a roller disco), as well as singing on most of the soundtrack. Donna Summer, who earned the title of the Queen of Disco, was influential during this period too, as was Barry White, whose deep, deep, luscious voice drew the ladies onto the dance floor.

I call Barry White's tunes from the disco era "baby making music" because they are seeeeeee-xy!

If you want to look at the work of some of the best disco songwriters, look to the songs of Paul Jabara ("The Main Event," "No More Tears," "Enough Is Enough," "Last Dance"); John Farrar ("Magic," "Have You Never Been Mellow," "A Little More Love"); and Barry Gibb ("Jive Talking," "Boogie Nights," "How Deep Is Your Love," "You Should Be Dancing"), who, along with his brothers Robin and Maurice, formed the group the Bee Gees. Not only did the Bee Gees write and sing almost the entire soundtrack to the hit movie *Saturday Night Fever,* but apparently over 2,500 artists have recorded their songs.[3] And finally Gamble and Huff, whose Philadelphia soul sound gave us great disco tunes ("The Love I Lost," "Bad Luck," and "Love Train").

Pop and Rock Music of the '80s (the Entire Decade)

The breakdown you would receive for this audition would say: "Bring in a 1980s pop/rock song." Shows in this category include:

> *Fame*
> *Footloose*
> *Rock of Ages*
> *Taboo*
> *The Wedding Singer*

Eighties pop and '80s rock are very different creatures. Eighties rock is Whitesnake and Def Leppard. Eighties pop is Whitney Houston, Cyndi Lauper, and Boy George. It is really good to know that these two extremes exist—the dark and the light. For great audition material, however, there are also tons of artists and groups, among them Journey, Foreigner, Pat Benatar, Heart, and Taylor Dayne, whose music falls in the territory right between the extremes. You can sing their songs for either pop or rock musicals auditions.

To research '80s songs, you need to look at the songwriters of this era, not just at the singers. Casting director Dave Clemmons has great taste in music. He feels that: "Most of the time, singer/songwriters write music for the quirkiness of their own voice, whereas people who are songwriters only, as opposed to singer/songwriters, write songs that are intended for vocally dynamic singers to sing."[4] Some of the songwriters I'm talking about are Carole Bayer Sager, Diane Warren, Jim Steinman, David Foster, Billy Steinberg, and Richard Marx, one of our favorite singer/songwriters who also wrote for other artists. Collaborators Barry Mann and Cynthia Weil, who began writing songs in the '50s, were still writing hits in the '80s! Who sang their songs in the '80s? The Pointer Sisters, James Ingram, Jeffrey Osborne, Peabo Bryson, and Chaka Khan did, to name a few. Look up all these amazing writers. The possibilities are endless.

I can't go another moment without talking about the '80s "yacht rock" phenomenon. This is for you in particular, boys. There was an actual video series in the 1990s that honored the soft rock writers of the '80s, emulating the gentleness of men and the way they bonded (picture yuppies out for a sail together). The list of who wrote and sang music in this genre is legendary: Kenny Loggins, Michael McDonald, Christopher Cross, Steely Dan, Hall and Oates, and Toto. Really, this music is incredible for auditions. For me, most of the singers from this era sang a perfect blend of pop and rock.

Contemporary Pop and Rock Music (Mid-1990s to the Present)

It is unfortunate that contemporary musical theater professionals tend to clump the last twenty years of rock music into one category. The breakdown for an audition for a contemporary production would ask you: "Bring in a contemporary pop/rock song," without drawing the same distinctions between pop and rock that I do. However, I encourage you to go further than the breakdown and embrace the distinctions. It's going to make it easier for you to make a jammin' selection that impresses.

Contemporary Rock Musicals

As a performer I have been fortunate to have appeared in a bunch of great rock musicals. I got the call to audition for a great rock musical called *Caligula* (based on the movie), and I had a hellacious cold. I mean, my voice was trashed—and I tend not to go to auditions when I'm sick. From experience I have found that the only emotion the casting director gets from me in my performance when I'm feeling ill is worry. But I went in this case because I knew everyone on the creative team, and I knew they would "hear" that I was under the weather. Well, let me tell you I went for it. I gave it everything I had, and I used the rawness in my voice to create a gritty, earthy rock sound. When I finished the song, they all said, "Oh my god, Sheri you sound amazing!" It was because my voice sounded so gritty and raw that day that I was able to give them exactly the sound they wanted.

Cindi Rush, the casting director who hired me for *Caligula*, says, "Rock is dirty, and messy, and edgy . . . your jeans aren't clean. It's the ache in the music that makes it rock. This ache is why rock stars are up all night; because it's so bad, there's not enough scotch in the world to cure this ill. Rock is showing us brokenness. The rock sound is earthy and grounded . . . People haven't showered in five days. It's down and it's dirty; it's to the floor."[5]

The following shows can be considered contemporary rock musicals:

American Idiot
Bloody Bloody Andrew Jackson
High Fidelity
Passing Strange
Rent
Rooms
Spiderman

What the creative teams are looking for when casting these shows is an authentic, emotionally raw sound. That rawness is present in so many different voices. Guys, if you are auditioning for *American Idiot*, remember that you can find the raw sound in everything from Nirvana to Pearl Jam, to the Clash and Chris Daughtry. Also, you have *got* to listen to Jeff Buckley. His *Grace* album is outrageous. And his music is right for so many different styles of rock musicals. There was a musical created with his music and Shakespeare's text called *The Last Goodbye,* which was done at Williamstown Theatre Festival in 2010. That's how great he was. Now, girls, if you look at some of the grittiest and most dynamic rock singers from this era, their works can be traced back to one woman, who both wrote and produced for them. Who is this quintessential songwriter for our time? The unbelievable Linda Perry of 4 Non Blondes. She also happens to be an incredible singer.

Look her up, darling. She's going to blow your mind.

Contemporary Pop Musicals

Pop musical theater auditions are where a lot of musical performers decide to sing a song from *The Wedding Singer.* No thank you, as that's the wrong era. But there are artists whose songs are awesome for an audition for a contemporary pop musical, including Britney Spears, Katy Perry, Lady Gaga, Justin Timberlake, Bruno Mars, and Beyoncé. An amazingly dynamic songwriter from our present era is Ryan Tedder, the former front man for OneRepublic. You won't believe the collection of pop singers he has written for, collaborated with, or produced: Hilary Duff, Leona Lewis, Jordin Sparks, and Beyoncé.

Of pop musicals, Cindi Rush says, "Pop has a lighter, more playful feel to it than rock. It doesn't necessarily have the 'middle of the night desperate need' that rock has, but it does have its own intensity. It's a younger, more untarnished intensity. Vocally it's a prettier sound, a cleaner sound. The focus is more on having a clean 'produced' feel, so the gritty edge doesn't exist."[6]

The shows that would fall into the contemporary pop genre include:

Altar Boyz
Bring It On
Brooklyn
In the Heights
Legally Blonde

Like '80s pop/rock music, contemporary pop/rock requires understanding the *extremes* of dark and light emotional expression. There is also a middle ground of rock songs that are fun and pop songs that have pain in them. When you are picking a song to audition with, you may be able to pull one from an artist whose music falls "right down the middle." Gwen Stefani of No Doubt is a pop artist who rocks. So are Pink, Christina Aguilera, Kelly Clarkson, Maroon 5, and Gavin DeGraw. Timeless talents like Phil Collins, Billy Joel, and Elton John are pop artists with a rock sound. Look at U2 and Sting. They are amazing sources of songs to sing.

Where Pop and Rock Blend in Contemporary Musicals

Casting directors sometimes will ask for "pop/rock songs" for musicals like:

Aida
Bare
Bat Boy
Billy Elliot
The Full Monty
Next to Normal (a crossover as it includes pop,
    rock, folk, *and* rock and roll)

Often, the creative teams of shows that fall in the zone between pop music and rock music love songs that also fall in between. Pop songs that are perfect in an audition for a pop musical can be just dreadful for *American Idiot* or *Bloody Bloody Andrew Jackson*. And rock songs that are perfect in an audition for a rock musical can be inappropriate for *Legally Blonde* or *In the Heights*. But many songs are hybrids of dark and light.

Spring Awakening, which is most definitely a rock musical, is also poetic. This leaves it open for your audition song to be a hybrid. It's not a pop/rock hybrid; it's really a folk/rock hybrid. During the auditions for the original production of *Spring Awakening,* the casting directors asked for songs by the Beatles, Bob Dylan, Joni Mitchell, and Simon and Garfunkel, because these artists are known to be exceptionally poetic. If you audition for *Spring Awakening* at some date in the future, remember that you could sing a song from one of these great artists, or you could sing a song from a contemporary songwriter/poet. I call these artists "the fairies." Singers like Tori Amos, Kate Bush, Bjork, Regina Spektor, Ingrid Michaelson, Sara Bareilles, and Rufus Wainwright are ethereal: they have a mystical quality about them but are not without exceptional storytelling ability. Both Tori Amos and Regina Spektor, in fact, are writing musicals of their own. This is where the light enters the darkness of rock.

There you have it: the different genres of rock musicals. Of course, our discussion of styles is not complete yet, because many tunes you would choose to sing for rock musical auditions are infused with other influences that are neither pop nor rock. Let's take a look at these styles for a moment.

Blues, Country, Gospel, R&B, and Folk

Styles outside of rock and pop are a tricky subject. The musical theater community clumps all of them into one category since not a lot of shows are *specifically* blues, gospel, country, R&B, or folk. This gross generalizing hurts me deep inside, as these musical genres are vastly different from one another and deserve our respect and understanding. Few producers of musicals would ask you to do a song in any of these four genres. But it is imperative that you study these styles. For although there aren't a lot of gospel, blues, folk, and country musicals, their influence is in *everything*. They flavor all of our music. Let me share what I can with you about their history . . .

Blues

Blues music was born in the Mississippi Delta after the Civil War, which may be why, by its very nature, it has a melancholy and sadness to it. Some of the great blues influences are Duke Ellington, Bessie Smith, Muddy Waters, B. B. King, John Lee Hooker, Johnny Winter, Stevie Ray Vaughn, Billie Holiday, Blues Traveler, Keb' Mo', Kenny Wayne Shepherd, Johnny Lang, and Adele. *Smokey Joe's Café, It Ain't Nothin' but the Blues,* and *Million Dollar Quartet* all give you the blues.

Country

Country music was cultivated in 1910 by Appalachian fiddle players. Really it is a blend of big band music, blues, Dixieland music, and jazz with different subcategories, like honky tonk, western, rockabilly, bluegrass, and the Nashville sound. Some great country influences are

Johnny Cash, Dolly Parton, Patsy Cline, Willie Nelson, John Denver, Garth Brooks, Billy Ray Cyrus, Alison Krauss, Reba McEntire, and the Dixie Chicks. Musicals like *The Robber Bridegroom, Pump Boys and the Dinettes,* and *Ring of Fire* ask for country music for their auditions.

Gospel

Gospel music's roots can be traced back to the eighteenth century and slavery in America. The traditional hymns that were slow in tempo and solemn in mood became spirituals, chants, call-and-repeats, shouts, and anthems. Gospel became a way that enslaved people communicated with God and one another in a language that was exclusively theirs.

I have the great honor of being a member of a gospel choir called Broadway Inspirational Voices. Michael McElroy, one of the greatest musical theater performers of our time, who is also a great teacher, created the gospel choir, and writes and arranges music. Michael says, "You have to understand gospel was a music born out of a people who had nothing but their music to get them through, and because of this there is blood in every note."[7]

Some of the great leaders in gospel music are Mahalia Jackson, Sister Rosetta Tharpe, Clara Ward, Shirley Caesar, the Edwin Hawkins Singers, Kirk Franklin, Daryl Coley, CeCe Winans, and Mary, Mary. You would do well to consider singing one of their songs if you are prepping an audition for *Leap of Faith, The Color Purple,* or *All Shook Up.*

Rhythm and Blues (R&B)

R&B is more of a marketing term than a specific musical genre. It has taken on several meanings since the early '40s. The term was initially used by record companies to describe music marketed to urban African Americans. The rock-beat style of jazz was its most defining characteristic, even as it morphed through the years into funk, soul, hip-hop, disco, Motown, pop, and the countless subgenres that these styles created. To this day, it has remained a blanket term for unclassifiable music that would otherwise be confusing to describe. "Hip-soul with gospel influences and disco-funk beats," for instance, is much more approachable when simply referred to as "R&B."

Who are some of the R&B singers you need to know about? You should familiarize yourself with Fats Domino, Chuck Berry, Della Reese, Sam Cooke, Michael Jackson, Prince, Patti LaBelle, Marvin Gaye, Aretha Franklin, and Teena Marie. As far as shows go, *In the Heights* and *Dreamgirls*, though vastly different, both have an R&B essence to them.

Folk

In 1961, folk music was an alternative to the Brill Building–Phil Spector–teen pop world embraced by socially active college students in the peace and civil rights movements. Folk themes include war, work, civil rights, economic hardship, and love. Folk lyrics are often satirical. Musicians in the folk tradition include Woody Guthrie; Joni Mitchell; Simon and Garfunkel; the Mamas and the Papas; Pete Seeger; Joan Baez; Bob Dylan; Peter, Paul and Mary; Harry Chapin; Shawn Colvin; Damien Rice; and Ani DiFranco. Folk-inspired musicals are *The Times They Are A-Changin',* *Floyd Collins,* and *Spring Awakening.*

Have a listen to the wonderful performers who sing all five of these alternative styles. They are just a few examples of the influences you can hear in any of the pop/rock genres and eras we've explored thus far.

Rock musicals, like people, come in all shapes and sizes. Next, let's check out the different ways they are conceived.

Pop/Rock Musicals Written by Famous Pop/Rock Artists

Aida, The Lion King, and *Billy Elliot* were composed by Elton John. *Tarzan,* by Phil Collins. The music for *Spring Awakening* was written by Duncan Sheik. Paul Simon wrote the music for *The Capeman. Dance of the Vampires* was co-written by Jim Steinman, who wrote songs for Meatloaf, Bonnie Tyler, Barry Manilow, Air Supply, and Celine Dion. Following in the footsteps of Burt Bacharach, these celebrated artists transported themselves from the recording studio into the theater. The reason why they found a home on the Broadway stage is that it is in a singer/songwriter's nature to express his feelings in a dramatic manner. And that's what theater does. The combination therefore makes perfect sense. For the most part, these artists' music is accessible to everyone. Their songs are not extreme like the rock songs in *American Idiot,* which are emotionally reckless in tone; and they're definitely not like *Rock of Ages,* which makes fun of the silliness of a bygone era.

For auditions for *Aida,* the producers asked actors to prepare a song that was not period specific, and that had a pop/rock sound that was, well, pop (meaning a sound that anyone could listen to, which would not be exclusive to any age or community). They wanted to hear something accessible, like the music of Elton John, Billy Joel, or even Bono (who wrote *Spiderman*)—undeniably brilliant, yet complex pop artists who write songs that are simple in sentiment.

When you audition for this type of show, you're neither interpreting poetry, nor banging your head like a rock star. This would be a good opportunity to look at each of these artists' body of work. It will give you a clear understanding that these kind of songs are fantastic to sing for *lots* of auditions for musicals written by pop writers.

Jukebox Musicals

The term "jukebox musical" means a musical created using songs from a songwriter's already existing canon and creating a story around these songs. Examples of jukebox musicals (and the artists they feature) are:

> *All Shook Up* (Elvis Presley)
> *The Buddy Holly Story* (Buddy Holly)
> *Good Vibrations* (the Beach Boys)
> *Jersey Boys* (Frankie Valli and the Four Seasons)
> *Lennon* (John Lennon)
> *Love, Janis* (Janis Joplin)
> *Mamma Mia!* (Abba)
> *Movin' Out* (Billy Joel)
> *Smokey Joe's Café* (Jerry Leiber and Mike Stoller)
> *The Times They Are A-Changin'* (Bob Dylan)
> *We Will Rock You* (Queen)
> *The Last Goodbye* (Jeff Buckley)

When auditioning for these musicals, you need to sing either a song from the featured artist (but preferably not a song from the show, unless they ask—and they'll usually ask you for that for the callback) or a song that is in the same style as the show.

Some jukebox musicals incorporate songs from many different artists, because they intend to celebrate an era. *Rock of Ages,* for instance, celebrates 1980s rock culture. *Priscilla, Queen of the Desert* celebrates the disco era. *Shout, Million Dollar Quartet, Beehive, Leader of the Pack,* and *Forever Plaid* celebrate the '50s and '60s. Because they are era specific, you need only to look at the essence of the era to make a song selection.

Concept Albums

The concept album came about because there was a switch in the format of recorded music in the late '50s and '60s. Music lovers went from buying single songs recorded by their favorite artists as "forty-fives," (small vinyl discs that made forty-five revolutions per minute on a turntable), to buying full-size long-playing vinyl discs, or LPs, (which made thirty-three and a half revolutions per minute on a turntable). Today these are known as record albums. When the opportunity to play many songs in a row arose, it allowed writers to explore creating a dramatic arc. Two bands that succeeded in making an album with a story built into it were Pink Floyd (*The Wall* and *Dark Side of the Moon)* and the Who (*Quadrophenia* and *Tommy*). These albums told dramatic stories through song.

An album of this nature has great potential to be dramatized onstage; however, it is a rare occurrence for one to find its way there. The only successful concept productions I am aware of are *Tommy* and *American Idiot*, (which was the first punk rock opera ever to make it to the Broadway stage).

Although Andrew Lloyd Webber is a musical theater writer, *Jesus Christ Superstar* could be considered a concept album. It had one of the greatest scores of all time, but the stage production doesn't translate as well as singing along to the album with your friends. I'm not entirely sure why it doesn't translate onstage, but I prefer to listen to the record (yes, I have a record player!) because it leaves so much to my imagination. That way I get to act out *all* the characters with my friends.

Sheri's Six Special Rules of Rock

Don't let this worry you, sweet pea. I promise that everything I am teaching will make sense in the end. The only reason I am creating "special" rules is that there really are no hard and fast rules to picking rock songs for an audition. Rock musicals are very new to the musical theater community, which is already over eighty years old. So these are my six loving suggestions.

Rule #1: Never Sing a Rock Song from a Rock Musical. Singing a rock musical number for a pop/rock audition is a big no-no. People holding rock auditions really don't like it. They would rather have a song from the radio.

I know, I know. Earlier on I said that an actor did a memorable audition when he sang "Gimme the Ball" from *A Chorus Line,* and now I'm telling you not to sing a song from a musical. Let me explain the contradiction. When the breakdown asks for a rock song, this should not mean you sing one from a rock musical. Why? Because you can't do with a song from a rock musical what the guy who sang "Gimme the Ball" did. He was able to transform a musical theater song to fit the '50s because it already hinted at the essence of old school R&B. It just is not possible to transform a song like "Take Me or Leave Me" from *Rent*, or "Good Morning Baltimore" from *Hairspray,* or something from *Mamma Mia* into another essence. They aren't as pliable. "Gimme the Ball" had rhythm, but it wasn't locked into a certain style.

I really believe that guy doesn't normally sing "Gimme the Ball" for his rock auditions. I am *certain* that's not his rock musical audition song. Songs that already exist in a musical were written to do what musical theater songs do. They're meant to move the plot forward. So the storytelling in rock songs is just plain different, and frankly what people would prefer to see.

Rule #2: Never Sing a Contemporary Pop Musical Theater Song. Another really big no-no is bringing a song from a legit contemporary musical to a pop/rock musical audition. There are outstanding pop musical theater writers, people such as Joe Iconis, Lowdermilk and Kerrigan, Pasek and Paul, and Ryan Scott Oliver. I love them all. I think Jason Robert Brown and Andrew Lippa are rock stars. For a contemporary musical theater audition, their music is a flawless choice. But you cannot bring these songs in for rock musicals because they come from musical theater storytellers. These songwriters are geniuses working in a different genre. They may want *you* to bring in a pop/rock song to audition for *them personally,* but they're musical theater folks, not top ten hitmakers.

Rule #3: Know Your Songwriter. If you walked into an audition room where I was behind the table and you said, "I'm singing 'Killing Me Softly' by Lauryn Hill," I would decide you were a dum-dum, because *I* know that Roberta Flack wrote and sang this song originally and Lauryn Hill covered it. This is information you know if you looked at the sheet music or researched the song on the internet.

When you go to an audition, know who wrote your song, know who sang it, and know who covered it. Not everyone sings music they wrote themselves. People often have songs written for them. It is impressive, cool, and professional to know the correct details. One time, a girl came and sang for me, saying, "Hi! I'm singing 'Let It Be' from the movie *Across the Universe.*" She literally had to pick me up off the floor. Granted she was not born yet when this famous song was written, but it really was a terrible sign of ignorance not to know the name of the most famous and popular songwriters of the twentieth century, John Lennon and Paul McCartney, who were half of the Beatles. I went online to find the sheet music for the song "Maybe This Time," and instead of saying "from the show *Cabaret,*" the sheet music says "from *Glee.*" *Glee* is a brilliant show; however, it may unfortunately be the culprit in situations like this!

Rule #4: Avoid Overdone Songs Like the Plague. It's impressive if you have chosen a good song. It's also important to be aware of which good songs are overdone in auditions—and to avoid them.

For example, let's look at "Alone" by Heart. When an actor comes in with this song, the people seated behind the table in the audition room think the following types of things (I know because they've told me so):

> I hear the intro and the "gate" goes down. I don't care about your voice because you are totally unconscious. The twenty-five girls standing in front of you sang "Alone." You know this because you hear it a million times at every single rock EPA you go to, but clearly you do not care that we are sick of hearing it, and you haven't searched the tremendous canon of music Heart has written for a different song that has just as broad a range, but has a better, cooler story in it, one that doesn't make me want to vomit. Instead, you've chosen to pick this song, and you are thinking, "Oh good, now I have my 'rock song.' I don't have to worry about this anymore."

One rock song does not cover all the different eras and genres. *Raaaarrrrrr!*

The fact is that if you sing a grossly overdone song and you are *amaaaaaazing,* then yes, they'll get over how much they hate the song. You have to be so amazing that your talent, vocal prowess, emotional connection, and storytelling richness transcend the song itself. Are you *that* amazing? If you aren't (or even if you are), why *not* have them say, "Wow, *great* song," because they rarely hear it *and* they loved your rendition.

Under no circumstances will you sing any of the following songs. Don't you dare! And for that matter, I want you guys to practice, interpret, and stage the songs I will offer as examples for teaching purposes in this book. Do *not* use them as your audition songs. Remember, *bazillions* of other actors will be reading this book and thinking they are having the same bright idea as you... and this handful of gems I use in the preceding chapters will become more overdone than this list will ever be!

"Alone" by Heart
"Somebody to Love" by Queen
"Total Eclipse of the Heart" by Bonnie Tyler
"Holding Out for a Hero" by Bonnie Tyler
"Open Arms" by Journey
"Tell Him" by the Exciters
"I'm with You" by Avril Lavigne
"Son of a Preacherman" by Dusty Springfield

"Gravity" by Sara Bareilles
"It's My Party" by Lesley Gore
"Heartbreaker" by Pat Benatar
"Let's Hear It for the Boy," by Deniece Williams
"Make You Feel My Love," covered by Adele, written by Bob Dylan
"Since I Don't Have You" by the Skyliners
"Where the Boys Are" by Connie Francis
"You Oughta Know" by Alanis Morissette
"I Don't Wanna Be" by Gavin DeGraw
"Stand by Me" by Ben E. King
"River" by Joni Mitchell

Now, this is my opinion. It is not what the casting directors have told me; it's something I stand by. Some casting directors agree with me. Others honestly don't care what song you pick. This advice is solely based on my experience of sitting in on numerous auditions and watching actor after actor choose these same songs out of lack of interest in exploring the other possibilities.

Why not choose to have the door *totally* open?

Rule # 5: Choose a Song That Most People Would Know. Make it easy for the creative team by doing a song that could bring back memories for them. If you sing a song that most people know, but perhaps haven't heard in a long while, they think, "Oh, I love that song! I haven't heard it in so long." They notice you and thank you with a callback for your exquisite rendition of a song they recognize and like. They'll be really open to you.

What if you really want badly to do a song they might not know? I love giving out lesser-known songs by Pink. Or if you wrote a song you want to sing and accompany yourself on the guitar? This is fine to do if the unfamiliar song meets two qualifications:

1. It is appropriate for the genre.

2. It is musically and lyrically clear and *simple.* If the song you do is complex or crazy in any way and the people behind the table don't know it, their first response will be, "What is this?" Then they've got a hard story to follow to respond to, and then they have to follow the melody and respond to that—and they don't even really know if you are singing the song *well,* because they don't know it.

In this case, you and your ability are the *last* thing they notice and respond to, which is a risk that I don't advocate when there are so many well-known songs available.

Rule #6: Remember That Anger Is Not an Emotion. For rock musical auditions, I've noticed that a lot of girls choose to sing angry songs, ones that are mean and have a lot of screaming in them. Now, I'm not saying you shouldn't sing anything painful. You absolutely should.

Pain is a beautiful emotion, and we, as an audience, want your pain . . .

But no one wants your nastiness.

There is room in your music to offer listeners a dynamic emotional ride without melting their faces off with the sound of your screaming rage.

When Carmel Dean, the musical director of *American Idiot*, sat together with me behind the audition table at an Equity chorus call, I asked her what she believes people think the essence of the music in *American Idiot* is. Carmel commented,

> People oftentimes see the description "rock musical" and think they need to come in with a loud, fast, and furious song, which they then proceed to scream their way through for everyone on the audition panel. What they forget is that they are still auditioning for a theater piece and there is a necessity to show emotional range—not just anger. I'm most impressed with people who come in with a traditional (or nontraditional) rock song and have a dramatic take on it. To me this is far more important than showing how high and loud they can belt.[8]

Always remember that your goal as a performer is for people to see who you are. That should come across underlying every song you sing and every line you speak.

I love Alanis Morissette. She is a revolutionary. When her early albums were produced, she broke through because she got women to confess their fury about the pain they feel when they are treated like shit. She is angry. She was so upset at Dave Coulier (that guy from *Full House*) for doing her wrong that she wrote *Jagged Little Pill*. The whole album is about him! A lot of girls come in and sing Alanis Morissette for obvious reasons. She is a leader in the contemporary rock movement. Her music is badass, and her voice, amazing.

Listen to "You Oughta Know."

You have a chance to share yourself with people in an audition. Do you want people to believe you're angry? I hope not.

Let's use my favorite contemporary rock artist of all time, Pink, as a contrasting example. She is an emotionally dynamic, exciting, thrilling, intelligent, and downright slammin' singer and songwriter. Now listen to "Nobody Knows."

Which song is the tastier of the two, Alanis or Pink?

Pink! Why? Because she is emotional, fun, earthy, raw, playful, dark, light, sensitive, vulnerable, wild, funny . . . and what I would call unbelievably dynamic.

Okay, now that the special rules are set, I'm ready to show you how to find a good song that takes the elements of story, character, and relationships into consideration.

The Importance of Context

Your casting breakdown, the same one that tells you the genre of song to prepare for the audition, also includes information about the character for which you are auditioning and small details about the plot of the show. Clearly, you need to do research when picking your song to make sure it shows off relevant facets of your personality. You would do this for your legit musical theater audition, wouldn't you? You would do it for a nonmusical audition, too, right? Right! I know you understand that this element makes a difference in your performance. That's why you succeed when you do. Right? Right!

So make the difference here. Do the research. If the soundtrack or the libretto of the musical exists, please look at it and listen to it—*all of it.* Don't just learn the song of the character for which you think you are right. Learn the character's relationship to everyone else in the show. Learn the story of the show. This is going to help your performance immensely. It will put the character you create in the "context" of the show.

If it's a new show, one where there's no music and no libretto to look at, investigate other avenues of information. Is it based on a movie? If so, watch the movie. Does the movie have a soundtrack? Listen to it.

If the score is written by a popular artist, listen to the artist's music. Learn about his or her voice.

Is there a website for the show? Look it up.

Has anyone on the creative team written other shows? For example, if you were auditioning for the first production of *Bring It On,* you would discover there was no music to listen to, as it is based on a nonmusical film. But you would know that the score was being written by Tom Kitt, who also wrote the Pulitzer Prize-winning show *Next to Normal* and *High Fidelity,* and orchestrated *American Idiot.* You know it's Lin-Manuel Miranda writing the music as well; he won a Tony Award for *In the Heights.* Look these creators up, and study the way they make music. You'll find, based on the past projects of these two men, that the music will be multidimensional with exciting beats and rhythm. After reviewing these things, you could safely assume that the show was going to be a contemporary high-energy pop musical. After all this, you'd then ask: what artists do you know whose music sounds like that? Or you could also go online and watch videos of competitive cheerleading and get great tunes from there.

Learn the creative team's point of view as best as you possibly can.

And do you want to know what will be *really* helpful—as in change-your-whole-life helpful? Go to the era or genre in which the show takes place. But how, you ask? Oh . . . I don't know . . . how about using the Internet? Everything you need to know is there for you. *Everything!*

Google the era, my darling. The information is at your fingertips. Here are some keywords and search phrases that can get you good results when you're looking for a song.

- ▶ One-hit wonders of...[type in the era]
- ▶ The greatest rock hits of the...[type in the era]
- ▶ Disco hit songs
- ▶ Women who rock
- ▶ Pop stars of the...[type in the era]

Instead of singing "Alone" by Heart, looking up the search phrase: "Heart greatest hits." These beautiful sisters of rock have been writing big, juicy hits for forty years. When you use different keywords, the search engines bring you lots of different videos, pictures, and songs that will make picking a tune so much easier.

This is my favorite idea: go to Pandora Radio (Pandora.com). Do you know Pandora? It is an Internet radio station that only plays the music an individual listener wants to hear. So you can create a personal radio station on your desktop computer or laptop featuring the music of an artist from every era who has had a top ten hit. Make yourself a Janis Joplin station. Make a Martha and the Vandellas station. Make a Whitney Houston Station and a Regina Spektor station. Then Pandora will play these artists' music and the music of other, similar artists. In this way, you have the opportunity to learn about singers you've never heard before, and listen to a million great songs. It's incredible.

VP Boyle is an acting teacher based in New York City who has spent some time as a casting director. In his opinion, an essential thing for you to think about while picking a tune for yourself is this:

> Everyone gets hung up on voice parts and high notes and forgets to think about the casting job at hand. A sparkly Disney-esque mix belter shouldn't sing boozy Janis Joplin. It doesn't make sense from a casting standpoint. The difference between James Blunt, the Barenaked Ladies, Justin Timberlake, and Steve Perry from Journey is huge. They are all pop or rock tenors, but their vocal style and sound is completely

different. All of their music could be fantastic options when auditioning for a rock musical—if they make sense on you. Only you know who you are. Be that person when you walk in the room and make sure that you are singing something that you can pull off with an authentic sound and emotional/physical/psychological landscape. If not, it all feels really weird and everyone in the room gets uncomfortable. We should feel energized by your performance and authenticity is the best thing you can consider when choosing your material. Not high notes or vocal ranges.[9]

Know your voice well enough to pick a great song for yourself.

If you notice you like an artist and they've had a few hits, buy their album! There is nothing like listening to a whole album. Joni Mitchell's *Blue*. Meatloaf's *Bat Out of Hell*. Christina Aguilera's *Stripped*. Laura Nyro's *Eli and the 13th Confession*. George Michael's *Listen Without Prejudice*. Led Zeppelin's *Mothership*. Carole King's *Tapestry*. The Police's *Synchronicity*. There are thousands upon thousands of albums to which you could listen. (I know, they're on CDs and MP3s now. Still, I want to call them albums.) You'd be learning how one singular human being expresses many feelings.

Do it now. You will grow so much.

How else could you find the right rock song? Well, try gender bending. Boys can sing girls' songs and girls can sing boys' songs. After all, Steve Perry is really an alto, not a tenor.

Where can you get the sheet music to these songs? There are tons of places online. Here's a short list of ones that I like:

▶ Musicnotes.com (In this site you can transpose music into your key. But please be careful to make sure the sheet music is an easy read for a pianist. Sometimes when it transposes notes, it puts it in a weird key. Check it out with a professional piano player before you bring it to an audition.)
▶ Sheetmusicdirect.com
▶ Sheetmusicplus.com
▶ FreehandMusic.com
▶ ColonyMusic.com
▶ Musicdispatch.com
▶ Hollywoodsheetmusic.com

Authenticity

Why is it so important to take this much care when choosing a song? In a word: authenticity. Don't you like people who are real? Aren't you repelled by people who bullshit you, or who don't seem to care? You don't trust those people. You don't want to be around them. Neither do casting directors and creative teams.

Think about how valuable you will be when you show up at an audition and give a performance as your authentic self that is also authentic to the genre. Again, the creative team will think, "Wow, this kid gets it! He understands the genre. He did the homework. He cares. He cares about this show. He cares about his experience—and our experience. Call him back."

Next, a lesson in the art of telling really *short* stories!

Now That I've Got a Rock Song, What on Earth Do I Do with It?

When auditioning for classic musical theater, the song you choose to sing has a clear story in it. It is meant to move an already exiting plot along because it is from a musical in which each song is a piece of a bigger puzzle. You understand now. We sing a condensed version of this preexisting story when we audition with a sixteen- or a thirty-two-bar cut.

Rock songs, however, are not *meant* to move a plot forward. They are a moment of someone's life. This moment, because it was never intended to be dramatized in a musical, is not linear in *any* way. So you are *totally* responsible for creating an arc—a progressing storyline—that doesn't originally *exist* in the song, all by yourself. *And* the song *needs* to be both vocally and emotionally exciting.

Oh . . . *and* you have to stay within the sixteen- or thirty-two-bar structure, depending on if you are a non-Equity or an Equity actor! So the cuts of your song need to be efficient. You need to get to the point. Short and sweet. This is especially important for Equity actors, because when you go to an EPA or an ECC you are "allowed" by Actors' Equity guidelines to sing a "whole" song. Don't you dare! Go in, knock their socks off, and then get the hell out of there. That way you leave them wanting more. They'll turn to you and say, "Wow that was great! Sing something *else* for us" or, the minute you leave the room, they'll turn to their assistant and say, "Call him back."

If your audition song is not short and sweet, they *will* grow bored and you *will* lose them. Please don't lose them. You need them to want you.

Typical Mistakes

As you know, I sat in on a bunch of Broadway rock musical auditions. I signed privacy clauses with all of the creative teams so I wouldn't ever divulge personal information about anyone in those rooms. I respect agents, musicians, actors, and creatives too much. But here are a few mistakes I saw that had to do with the arrangements singers were using. And here's what people did that reflected poorly on them.

The sheet music as a whole was a *mess*. Most of the time the artists who wrote the songs did not transcribe their own music; the publishers of their sheet music did. So the sheet music the actors were handing to the piano player was not an accurate reflection of the songs we hear on the radio—not on any level. What I saw was the singer at war with the accompaniment. Which is going to win—the piano or the voice?

If actors sang a song off the radio, the cuts were totally wrong. They'd start at the beginning, and then go to the bridge, and just before the best part of the song had arrived, they'd stop, because it was the end of their sixteen-bar or thirty-two-bar "allotment." Man, what a letdown!

People sang a cappella because they didn't even *have* a rock song. They didn't have *any* sheet music at all. One girl, who actually was a very good singer, tried to manipulate the casting team into believing this was a good idea, by saying, "I would *love* to sing my song a cappella for you." They told her it was okay, because they *had* to accept what she was offering. That's all she had. I thought, "But this isn't *American Idol,* you guys! And don't bullshit me, lady!"

I asked the casting person how long this actor and the other actors who sang a cappella had known about the audition. She told me they'd had a full month.

Raaaaaaaarrrrrrrrrr!

Another big mistake was that no one knew how to start his or her song—*no one.* The first three or four measures of every single person's songs were a disaster area. These are the moments you get to *grab* their attention so you can keep it! Those should be your strongest and most focused measures.

And the endings . . . I know it says "repeat and fade" at the end of the sheet music of most rock songs. But what happened over and over was that the performers didn't know how to create an ending, so they just stopped singing altogether. Then the accompanist had to decide *for them* how to end it. As a result, the last moment never felt complete. The story was never complete.

I sat in on one audition where a girl in the community who is talented, sang her song, and then, when it was time for the song to end, shouted, "And now the song stops!"

Really? And now the song stops?

I wanted to shout back, "Darling, why don't *you* stop it?"

One person came in with the song "Different Drum" by Linda Ronstadt and the Stone Poneys. She had a right-sized cut, but the coach with whom she worked (definitely a legit player of some kind) had arranged a key modulation, and a big section of riffing that ended on a high note. That riff had nothing to do with the meaning of the song, which is about a girl who doesn't want to let a guy know how much he has affected her. That sentiment wants some tears to be fought, not a big splashy ending!

Thank God I'm here to help.

In this chapter, I'm going to take the original versions of a handful of well-known rock songs, show you how to cut and arrange them, and then show you the final, cut versions. This way you will be able to see the types of simple stories you can end up with that are so great for auditions when you've got all the right elements in play within your song at the same time. Really, an audition song can be magic if you let it.

Guess what else. These are the same sweet songs I'm going to use to teach you everything you need to know about how to act a rock song later on in the book. So I suggest that you start getting to know them. Listen to them on your iPod or MP3 player until they seem familiar to you if they aren't already. Here's our list.

"Let It Be" recorded by the Beatles
"In Love with a Girl" recorded by Gavin DeGraw
"A Song for You" recorded by Donny Hathaway
"Please Mr. Postman" recorded by the Marvelettes
 "What's Up?" recorded by 4 Non Blondes
"So Emotional" recorded by Whitney Houston

As a friendly reminder, these must not be your new audition songs.

The Four Basic Structures of an Audition Song

Songs have several components that make up their form. There is the verse, which sets up the scenario; the chorus, which is the body of the story; and the bridge, which heightens the story and takes it from one place to the next (like a real bridge). There are also many variations on this form. A standard pop form, which is the form of rock song we typically use for auditions, starts with a verse, goes into the chorus, goes back to the verse, then back into the chorus, then into the bridge, and back to the chorus one more time. But, honey, that's way too long for an audition song.

There are four basic structures or patterns of arrangement that a successful audition song uses to tell a full-blown story in sixteen or up to thirty-two measures of music. The key here is that we are looking for the story as it is told through the lyrics and through the emotions of the musical underpinnings.

1. Verse into the chorus
2. Bridge into the chorus
3. Bridge into the verse
4. Verse into the bridge into the chorus

Let's have a look at each of these patterns in order. Ready?

Pattern 1: Verse into the Chorus

Here's something important for you to know. In general, the only time you should begin the song at the real beginning is if the first verse is short, and if it is the beginning of a short story in which the verse goes right into the chorus. Do not do a second verse after that first one. Do not repeat the same verse twice. Go right into the chorus. Once through a particular section of the melody will do for your audition. If you go back to the verse again, the folks behind the table are going to wonder, "Why are you taking me back here? I was just here twenty seconds ago."

Casting director Cindi Rush says, "We don't need to know what has gone on before this song, and we don't need to know what's going to happen after it, so we don't need extra information. We don't need the B plot. Therefore we don't need the second verse and we don't need the fourth bridge. Actors should just be in the moment they're in."[1]

Looking at the song "Let It Be," which was composed by Paul McCartney and recorded by the Beatles, you can easily see that the chorus—sung straight through once—naturally repeats the phrase "Let it be/let it be/let it be/let it be/whisper words of wisdom/let it be" twice. That means, the second time around needs some good old-fashioned sprucing up; something juicy and delicious. If you intend to repeat something, you had better alter it in a way that lifts the audience emotionally and takes them somewhere. It must be important if you say it twice.

Here is "Let It Be" as it is in its original form.

Let It Be

Words and Music by
JOHN LENNON and PAUL McCARTNEY

When I find my-self in times of trou-ble Moth-er Ma-ry comes to me.
Speak-ing words of wis-dom, let it be. And
in my hour of dark - ness, she is stand-ing right in front of me

1

2

3

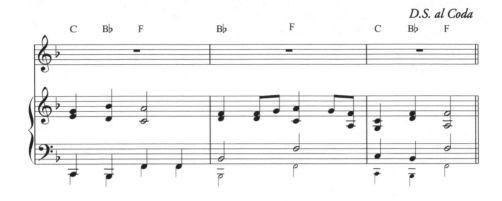

2. And when the broken hearted people living in the world agree.
   There will be an answer, let it be.
   For though they may be parted there is still a chance that they will see
   There will be an answer, let it be.
   Let it be, let be, let it be, let it be.
   There will be an answer, let it be.

(3rd time) Instrumental

4. And when the night is cloudy there is still a light that shines on me,
   Shine until tomorrow, let it be.
   I wake up to the sound of music - Mother Mary comes to me,
   Speaking words of wisdom, let it be.
   Let it be, let it be, let it be, let it be.
   Whisper words of of wisdom, let it be.

4

Now, have a look at the arrangement of "Let It Be" after a teeny bit of sprucing. Of course, my changes are only a suggestion. Ultimately, you'll use your own creativity.

From the handwritten notes, you can see that I suggest asking for a "bell tone" to start the song on the first page. By this I mean the accompanist will give you your "starting note," and then you will start the song. The song naturally begins with you, with no musical introduction.

As you can see, the melody line is written into the accompaniment. This will be the case 95 percent of the time. When you start to work with and audition with professional rock accompanists, they will absolutely know not to play the melody line, but till then you'll want to write at the top of the page, "no doubling the melody line on the piano," and very casually point to it, and say, "I don't need the melody line, thanks so much." My hope is whoever plays "Let It Be" knows not to play the melody line at all here, so I won't write it on this sheet music, but I will be doing it for another tune or two in the chapter. So keep an eye out for it!

On the third page, I have flagged a riff of my own creation, and instruct the pianist to "play the accompaniment fully." This music will really soar with your voice when you also notate the crescendo and the decrescendo at the beginning and the end of the riff section. I then bring the song back to a simple place by asking for sparse supporting chords. Notice the song ends like a sentence that reaches punctuation, rather than repeating and fading or going into a second verse.

It is super important to create a simple arrangement, one that is sparse instrumentally and that builds in intensity, while it properly supports and complements the voice of the singer. The arrangement *has* to sound great on the piano, my friend. So please find a piano player or a musical director who understands rock and pop songs, and ask this professional musician, this artist, to arrange the song for you and notate it on the sheet music. Remember to please rehearse the arrangement with this accompanist so that you know what you need to ask for at your audition.

You don't have to use my riff. Make up your own. Treat the song like jazz. Know what the original structure is so that you can leave it and come back to it. Always respect its boundaries. This song is so simple and beautiful. It actually doesn't need you to do anything fancy vocally—and emotionally it doesn't *want* a riff fest. But I wrote in a riff as a suggestion, so that you would know where one could be placed and how it could serve you in an audition song. The song *wants* to remain true to its nature. Please let it.

A rule of thumb: never ever riff because you want to show off.

Note: You do not have to write your vocal improvisations into the sheet music for the accompanist. If the music for the accompaniment is the same after you've created the riff, it does not require you to adjust it. I included the riff here merely for the sake of our discussion of where it should be.

Let It Be

Ask for a "C" bell tone
Slow tempo

Words and Music by
JOHN LENNON and PAUL McCARTNEY

1

2

*Ask for this section to be played fully

| 2., 4.

Bb F Gm7 F C Dm7

Let it be____ let it be, le - et____ it be,____

let it be.____

*Ask for sparse, supporting chords

C   Bb   F Gm7 F   End

Whis-per words___ of wis - dom, let it be.____

3

2. And when the broken hearted people living in the world agree.
   There will be an answer, let it be.
   For though they may be parted there is still a chance that they will see
   There will be an answer, let it be.
   Let it be, let be, let it be, let it be.
   There will be an answer, let it be.

(3rd time) Instrumental

4. And when the night is cloudy there is still a light that shines on me,
   Shine until tomorrow, let it be.
   I wake up to the sound of music - Mother Mary comes to me,
   Speaking words of wisdom, let it be.
   Let it be, let it be, let it be, let it be.
   Whisper words of of wisdom, let it be.

4

Does it make sense why I made a variation on it? It's subtle and yet dynamic. Here's the final audition version.

Let It Be

Words and Music by
JOHN LENNON and PAUL McCARTNEY

1

2

2. And when the broken hearted people living in the world agree.
   There will be an answer, let it be.
   For though they may be parted there is still a chance that they will see
   There will be an answer, let it be.
   Let it be, let be, let it be, let it be.
   There will be an answer, let it be.

(3rd time) Instrumental

4. And when the night is cloudy there is still a light that shines on me,
   Shine until tomorrow, let it be.
   I wake up to the sound of music - Mother Mary comes to me,
   Speaking words of wisdom, let it be.
   Let it be, let it be, let it be, let it be.
   Whisper words of of wisdom, let it be.

4

Pattern 2: Bridge into the Chorus

For this second demonstration of how to create a sixteen-bar song arrangement, we'll look at the song "In Love with a Girl" written and performed by Gavin DeGraw. It's a perfect example of why it's better sometimes to start at the bridge rather than with the first verse. You see, this song has a long, slow buildup of intensity. So the best thing to do is start your audition from an energetic part of the song—not the most energetic, but not the least energetic either. The bridge is the place to start because it is energetically right in the middle. Arranging it this way you can quickly build to the most energetic place, and once you reach the peak, you can "bring it home" with the chorus.

Since the audition cut of the song starts at the bridge, the suggestions for the cut I have just described are handwritten inside of the original sheet music.

In Love with a Girl

Moderate hard-driving rock ♩ = 84

Words and Music by
GAVIN DeGRAW

1. So man-y peo-ple gon-na say that they want you
2. Out the man-y bro-ken back doors and win-dows

to try to get you think-in' they real-ly____ care.
through the val-ley of the love of the____ lost

1

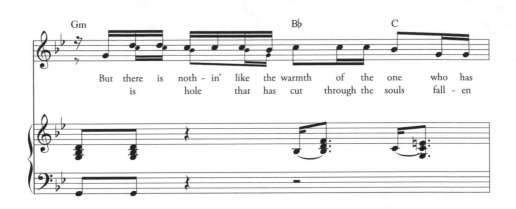

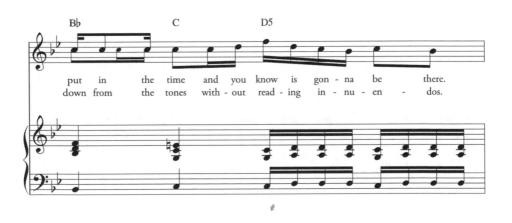

2

See? The song is pretty long!

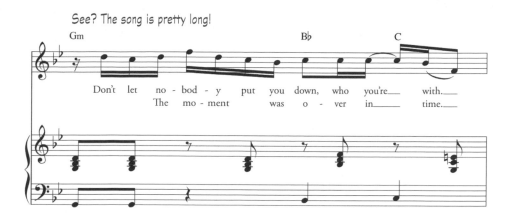

Don't let no-bod-y put you down, who you're___ with.___
The mo-ment was o-ver in___ time.___

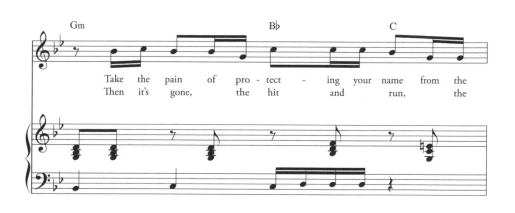

Take the pain of pro-tect - ing your name from the
Then it's gone, the hit and run, the

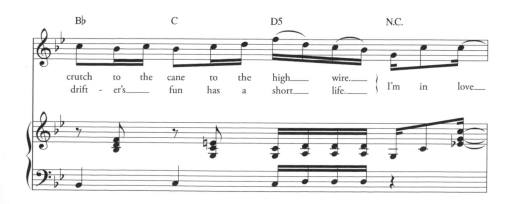

crutch to the cane to the high___ wire.___ I'm in love___
drift-er's___ fun has a short___ life.___

3

_____ with a girl who knows me bet-ter. Fell_____ for the wom-an just when I met her._ Took

my sweet time when I was bit-ter._ Some-one un - der-stands._ And she knows

_____ how to treat a fel-la right. Gives_____ me that feel-in' ev - 'ry night. Wants

4

to make love when I wan-na fight. Now some-one un-der-stands me._____ I'm in

love with a__ girl._____
I'm in love with.__

I'm in love with a__ girl._____

I'm in love with.__

6

to be warm and wel-come._____ to___ be held and shel-tered. I'm in love

Here comes the
(Chorus) !

___ with a girl who knows me bet-ter. Fell____ for the wom-an just when I met her.___ Took

my sweet time when I was bit-ter.___ Some-one un-der-stands._____ And she

7

8

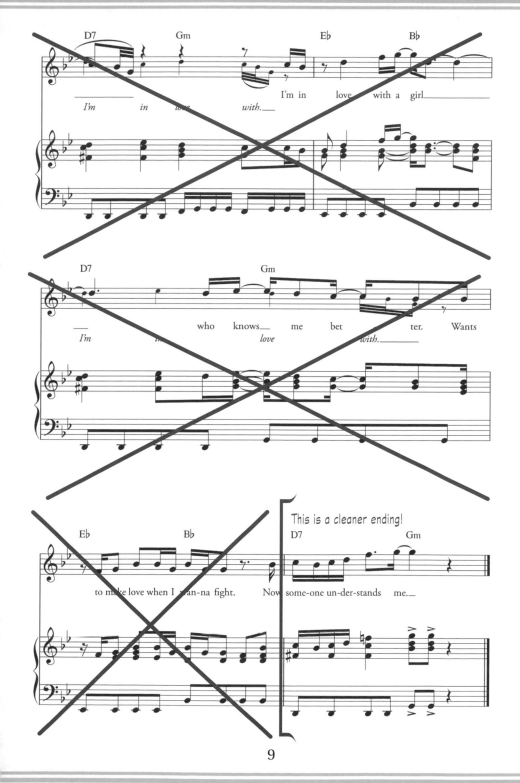

Now, take a look at the cut version. We've reduced six pages of sheet music to fit on three magical pages. I notated an instruction for the accompanist to start with a bell tone. Again, I'd encourage you to ask the accompanist to leave out the melody line.

Bridge into chorus in sixteen bars is an awesome cut that works well. You need to recognize that this modest type of arrangement is really all you need musically to lay the groundwork for an impressive audition. You can be a great singer and a wonderful actor, but the cuts you make *create* the story from which you will *express* character. Trust that this is enough. As we go on in the book, you'll realize this cut is, indeed, perfect based on what we do when acting it.

Your finished product should look like this.

In Love with a Girl

No doubling the melody line on piano
"F" bell tone

Words and Music by
GAVIN DeGRAW

1

2

Some - one un - der - stands._____ And she knows how to treat a fel - la right. Gives____ me that feel - in' ev - 'ry night. Wants to make love when I wan-na fight. Now some-one un-der-stands me.___

End

3

Pattern 3: Bridge into the Verse

Although I won't be using this song as a teaching tool later in the book, it was necessary for me to show you what the structure of a song is like if your arrangement starts at the bridge and then goes into a verse. This does not require a big cut and pasting experience, so I am showing you the full song, and where the cut happens. You don't need to do anything to it.

Here is one of my favorite tunes in the world, "A Song for You," written by the great Leon Russell and originally sung by Donny Hathaway.

A Song for You

Slowly ♩ = 66

Chorus

Words and Lyrics by
LEON RUSSELL

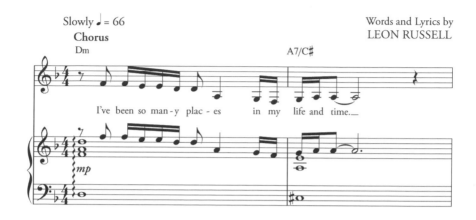

I've been so man-y plac-es in my life and time.

I've sung a lot of songs. I've made some bad rhyme. I've

act-ed out my love in stag-es with ten thou-sand peo-ple watch-in'.

1

but we're a-lone now and I'm sing-ing this song___ for you.___

I know your im-age of me___ is what I hope to be.___

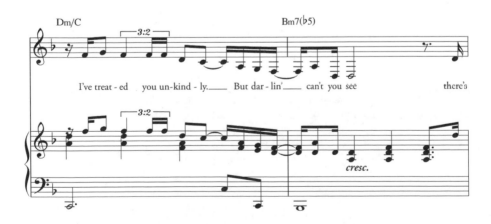

I've treat-ed you un-kind-ly.___ But dar-lin'___ can't you see there's

2

no one more im-por-tant to___ me,___ dar-lin' can't you please see through me?_

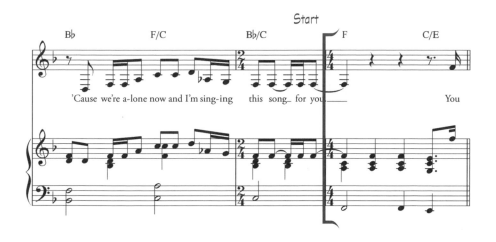

Start

'Cause we're a-lone now and I'm sing-ing this song_ for you____ You

Bridge

taught me pre-cious se-crets of the truth_____ with-hold-ing noth - ing.

You came out in front and I was hid-ing_____ but

now I'm so much bet-ter, and if my words___ don't come to-geth-er,

lis-ten to the mel-o-dy___ 'cause my love is in there hid - ing._____

4

I love you in a place where there's no space or time. I

love you for my life.____ You are a friend of mine.__ And

when my life__ is o-ver__ re-mem-ber when we were to-geth-er.__

5

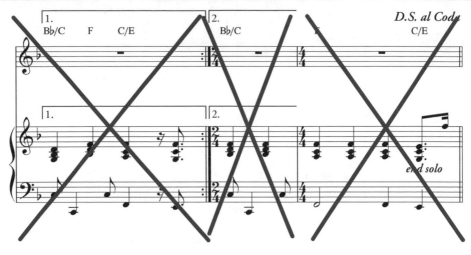

6

A Second Verse–Chorus Arrangement

Have you ever noticed that certain songs, which otherwise are great to listen to, kind of flat-line? They never build into anything exciting musically and feel like they could use a good climb in them? "Please Mr. Postman," which was originally recorded by the Marvelettes, is that kind of song. If you can find a story somewhere in the song and it's got the right essence for the time period and a character you could potentially portray, the question, sweet cookie, is why can't you create that build *yourself*? To transform it into a great audition piece, all you have to do is listen. Is there a great story in there? Is there any cool riffing by the backup singers going on? Could you bring the background of the song to the foreground to make the story that already exists stronger?

Listen to different versions of the song. It was covered by the Carpenters…*and* the Beatles! All very different versions. Can you pull cool elements from any of the different interpretations? I loooove that Karen Carpenter says "stop" at the beginning of her version of the song, as opposed to "wait." So by the time the second "wait" happens, the beginning feels really urgent! I'm gonna use it!

At first glance on the original sheet music, which was five pages long, "Please Mr. Postman" needed a lot of work. One of the things I loved about the Marvelettes' version was the handclaps at the beginning of it. You'll see how I circled these on the first page to reserve them as an element for later in my arrangement. At the bottom of the third page, I noted for myself that even though I was finding an actable story, it wasn't a bold enough story for a really juicy audition. Just waiting for the postman to come has no intensity or dramatic conflict in it.

Then you can see how the vibrant storyline emerges on the fourth page. Yeah, this is what I am talking about! The lyrics where I intend to start my arrangement begin emphatically with the command "Stop!" This story is intriguing. "Wait!" Leading into *this* story, she's got the postman's attention, and she's got lots to say. Now we're on to something.

I looked for a great spot to insert handclaps, somewhere I could add a modest riff, and also looked for what would be the best ending to my story. Good news, the ending was already there. As you'll see, I marked all of those on my original version of the sheet music.

Please Mr. Postman

Words and Music by ROBERT BATEMAN,
GEORGIA DOBBINS, WILLIAM GARRETT,
FREDDIE GORMAN and BRIAN HOLLAND

1

2

3

4

5

6

As I began cutting and pasting lines in order to clarify my personal vision of the song and begin establishing the arrangement on paper, you can see how my cut not only picks out a short clear story inside of this story, but also combines the backup part with the lead part to accentuate the feeling of the time period.

As I like to do, I created a bell tone instruction for the first bar on page one. I also immediately struck out the melody line, as I do not—under any circumstances—want the piano player in the audition to play the same notes as the one I am singing. Remember, that's one of the mistakes people typically make. You'll notice how in a certain place it seemed too congested, so I made notes to simplify it visually. I also decided to add the handclaps back in and to end the song up on a D rather than an F.

Take a look at my intermediate edits of the sheet music.

Please Mr. Postman

Words and Music by ROBERT BATEMAN,
GEORGIA DOBBINS, WILLIAM GARRETT,
FREDDIE GORMAN and BRIAN HOLLAND

1

I wanna fiddle with this accompaniment. It feels too full.

make me feel bet - ter by leav - ing me a

card or a let - ter. Please, Mis-ter Post - man, look and see; is there a

let - ter, oh, yeah,___ in your bag for me? You know, it's

2

3

Finally, look closely at "Please Mr. Postman" as I fancied it up. This is the version you'll put in your audition book and give to the piano player at the audition. I had a gorgeous arrangement made that is clear, concise, and on two pages. My friend Mark Fifer did it. Take a look.

Politely ask the accompanist if he's game to drop out and do the handclaps for you. This creates big-time '50s essence. Afterwards you must thank him very, very much for playing along with you and going the extra mile. If he doesn't seem willing, do them yourself. Practice it both ways so you won't be surprised.

Please Mr. Postman

Words and Music by ROBERT BATEMAN,
GEORGIA DOBBINS, WILLIAM GARRETT,
FREDDIE GORMAN and BRIAN HOLLAND

1

make me feel bet - ter by leav-ing me a card or a let - ter.

Please Mis-ter Post - man look and see, is there a let - ter, oh yeah, in your

bag for me? You know, it's been so ___ long, yeah, ___ since I

heard from this boy-friend of mine. You'd bet - ter

2

wait a min- ute, wait a min- ute. Oh,_ you'd bet-ter wait a min- ute, wait a min- ute.

Please, Mis-ter Post - man!_____ De-

liv - er de let - ter, the soon-er de bet - ter.

3

Pattern 4: Verse into the Bridge into the Chorus

Let's look at another formula for turning a rock song into an actable audition piece. "What's Up?" a contemporary rock tune written by Linda Perry, lead singer of 4 Non Blondes, released in 1992 was destined to be a classic. Hopefully you've looked her up by now. If not, go to YouTube and play this song immediately. Linda Perry is an important songwriter with whom budding chick rock singers in particular should get familiar. This gorgeous creature has written and produced songs for Pink ("Get the Party Started"), Christina Aguilera ("Beautiful"), Courtney Love ("Mono"), and Gwen Stefani ("What Are You Waiting For?"). For an audition, this song features a quintessential contemporary rock sound that also tells an awesome story.

What's Up?

Words and Music by
LINDA PERRY

1. Twen-ty-five years and my life is still___

1

try-in' to get up that great big hill__ of__ hope__ for a des-ti-na-

-tion. I real-ized quick-ly, as I knew I should, that this world

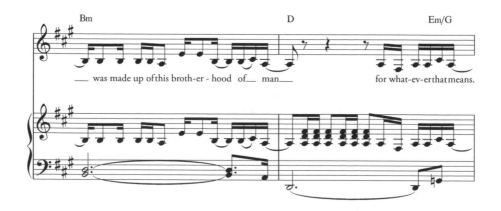

__ was made up of this broth-er-hood of__ man__ for what-ev-er that means.

2

Bridge

And so I cry some-times when I'm ly-ing in bed___ just to

get it all out,__ what's in___ my head, and I and I'm feel-ing a lit-tle pe-cu -

- liar. And so I wake in the morn-ing and I step out-side___ and I

3

take a deep breath and I get___ real high. And I scream from the top of my lungs, "What's go-in' on?"

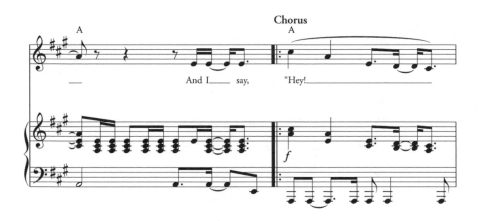

Chorus

___ And I___ say, "Hey!___

Hey!"___ I said, "Hey!___ What's go-in' on?"

5

Twen-ty-five years and my life is still___

6

try - in' to get up that great big hill___ of___ hope___

for a des - ti - na - tion.___

Fine

Fine

Verse 2
And I try, oh my God do I try.
I try all the time
In this institution.
And I pray, oh my God do I pary.
I pray every single day
For a revolution.

(To Bridge and Chorus.)

7

I was sitting in an audition and someone sang "What's Up" while accompanying herself on guitar. She did the entire song, and, although it's a stellar song, it is too damn long for an audition. It needs to be cut, as I have begun to do in the intermediate example below. The other thing I want to add in here is, you remember we talked about starting a song sparsely, to give the music a simpler, lower-intensity starting place so that there will be a higher-intensity place to build toward? Well, this cut—the verse to the bridge to the chorus—is the actual song once through. Look at the song, as I love to sing it.

You'll observe on the first page that I am going to begin in the sixth measure. I have circled the chords here as an instruction of what I mean by chord changes. I will begin my version of the song *colla voce,* which means "follow my voice."

On the third page, in the margin I write, "Rhythm begins (light pulse)," as an instruction to the piano player. Then, on the fourth page, I indicate, "Play heavy backbeats." I will point these notations out to him before beginning my performance at the audition. For myself, on the fifth page I write in the riff I intend to do. Again, this is just an example; it's for you, not the accompanist. You'll notice on the bottom of the fifth page and the top of the sixth page of the sheet music that I cross out several measures that would normally lead the singer back to sing the second verse of the song. In my audition version, I do the song once through from beginning to end. With our arrangement, it naturally takes the melody line out of the music, so no need to ask the accompanist to leave it out. Take a look at this example.

What's Up?

Words and Music by
LINDA PERRY

I wanna know "what's up" with all this piano in the beginning!

Slowly ♩ = 63

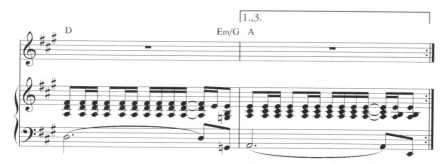

Chord changes only (no pulse), colla voce
(which means, "Follow my voice"). You take
the lead.

Let's start it simple.

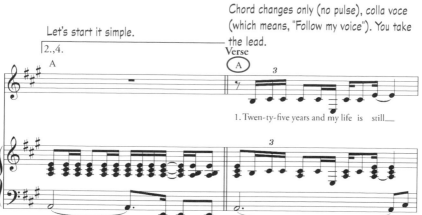

1. Twen-ty-five years and my life is still___

1

try-in' to get up that great big hill of hope

for a des-ti-na-

These are chord changes.

- tion.

I real-ized quick-ly, as I knew I should, that this world

was made up of this broth-er-hood of man

for what-ev-er that means.

2

Rhythm begins (light pulse)

Bridge

And so I cry some-times when I'm ly-ing in bed___ just to get it all out,___ what's in___ my head, and I and I'm feel-ing a lit-tle pe-cu - liar. And so I wake in the morn-ing and I step out-side___ and I

4

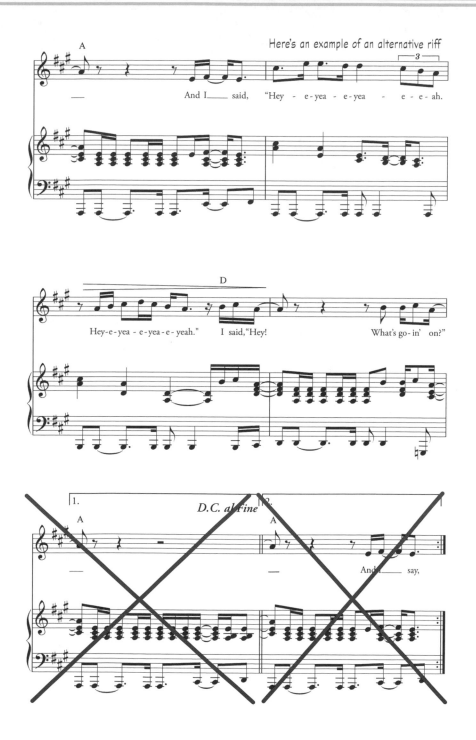

Bring this baby back home!

Slower ♩ = 58

Back to just chords

Twen-ty-five years and my life is still___

mp

6

try – in' to get up that great big hill_____ of_____ hope_____

_____ for a des – ti – na – tion._____

Verse 2
And I try, oh my God do I try.
I try all the time
In this institution.
And I pray, oh my God do I pary.
I pray every single day
For a revolution.

(To Bridge and Chorus.)

7

Here is what the audition version of the sheet music should look like.

What's Up?

Words and Music by
LINDA PERRY

1

get it all out, what's in___ my head, and I and I'm feel-ing a lit-tle pe-cu -

- liar. And so I wake in the morn-ing and I step out-side___ and I

take a deep breath and I get___ real high. And I scream from the top of my lungs, "What's go-in' on?"

3

Play heavy backbeats

Chorus

And I___ say, "Hey!_____

Hey!"_____ I said, "Hey!___ What's go-in' on?"

And I___ said, "Hey!_____

4

5

Let me say again, the riff I wrote in could be anything. I wrote it so I could create an emotional climb musically. But please, don't ever add a riff just to show off. If you do it, you have to be able to justify it with your acting.

A Second Verse–Bridge–Chorus Arrangement

The '80s are so distinctive in style, and there are so many shows coming out now that are based in the '80s, that it would be a shame not to include a song from that era here. My choice is "So Emotional," made famous by Whitney Houston, which, like "What's Up?," follows the dramatic arc of verse–bridge–chorus.

So Emotional

Words and Music by
BILLY STEINBERG and TOM KELLY

I've been hear-ing your heart-

1

-beat in-side of me; I keep your pho-to-graph be - side my bed.__

G   A   Em7

Liv-ing in a world of fan - ta - sies.__ I can't get you out of my head.

I've been wait-ing for the phone to ring all night

2

why you wan-na make me feel___ so good. I got a love of my own,

___ ba - by; I should-n't get so hung up on you.___ I re-

mem-ber the way___ that we touch.___ I wish___ I did - n't like___ it so

3

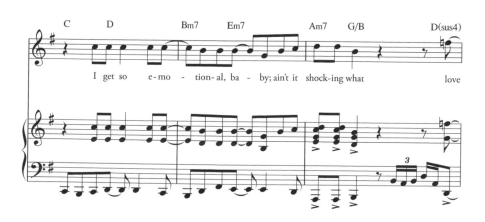

4

Verse 2
I gotta watch you walk in the room, baby;
I gotta watch you walk out.
I like the animal way you move,
And when you talk I just watch your mouth.

Oh, I remember the way that we touch;
I wish I didn't like it so much.

Here is an intermediate version of this tune. Notice how I have streamlined it. You can see that the introduction was shortened to two measures, repeated. You do not need to have a long introduction. That would be a waste of your precious time. The second verse was also marked for elimination so that the singer could go directly from the first verse into the bridge, and from there directly into the chorus.

You'll notice that I have made notes about the bass line. If I were to do this song in one of my auditions, I would want a simpler bass because it's actually kind of hard to play!

Take a look.

So Emotional

Words and Music by
BILLY STEINBERG and TOM KELLY

1

- beat   in-side of me;   I   keep your pho-to-graph be - side   my bed.__

G   A   Em7

Liv-ing in a world of   fan - ta - sies.__   I can't get   you   out of my head.

We definitely don't need the second verse!

I've   been   wait-ing for the phone to ring   all   night

2

3

4

Verse 2
I gotta watch you walk in the room, baby;
I gotta watch you walk out.
I like the animal way you move,
And when you talk I just watch your mouth.

Oh, I remember the way that we touch;
I wish I didn't like it so much.

5

When you listen to Houston's version of this song, you'll hear her do an amazing riff that was not written into the sheet music originally. It's such a fabulous riff that I always have one of my beautiful musical directors, Brad Simmons, add it into the material I use. Now it's there for you to use.

It is important for you to listen to the details of the song as it was originally produced. Listen for the cool vocal stuff that hasn't necessarily made it onto the page. Listen to the backup singers. Listen to the musical instruments. Then make a point of taking the juicier route through the song vocally. Use the biggest ending.

If the second verse is cooler than the first, perform that one. If the variation of the bridge is cooler after the second verse, perform that one.

As a general rule of thumb, in my arrangements I keep the first page of my song intact. I don't do cuts and pastes there because I feel, in general, that it is good to give the pianist as many visual clues as possible at the beginning. Even if I do rearrange a song, I keep the title, the name of the composer and lyricist, and leave in any crossed-out measures. If they need help getting a sense of the music, they could look at all of the above for clues. The melody line is written into the accompaniment, so this is a great place to ask for it to be left out.

Take a look at the final audition version of "So Emotional."

So Emotional

Words and Music by
BILLY STEINBERG and TOM KELLY

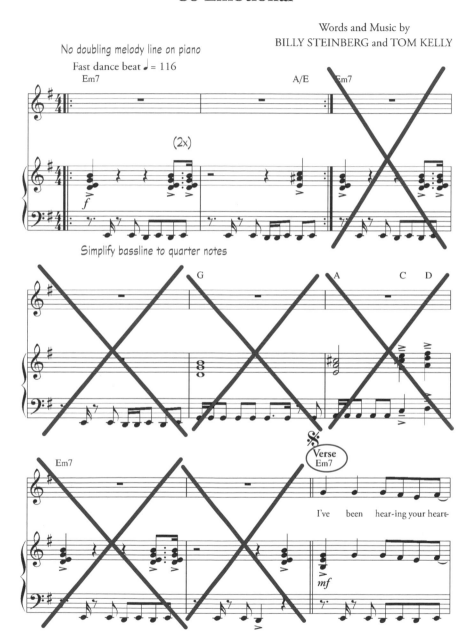

1

2

3

Verse 2
I gotta watch you walk in the room, baby;
I gotta watch you walk out.
I like the animal way you move,
And when you talk I just watch your mouth.

Oh, I remember the way that we touch;
I wish I didn't like it so much.

When you translate your intentions to the pianist correctly, you give them room. If your arrangement is a complicated cut-and-paste job, like the rearrangements we did of "Please Mr. Postman," then yes, do get a clean arrangement made.

The songs we've been discussing in this chapter represent four ways to cut and arrange music for an audition. When I hold a rock musical audition class, I generally arrange two songs for every student. That's twenty songs. In an advanced class, I arrange forty songs. Although there are only six songs here, these songs are good models.

Whether your song arrangements go verse into chorus, bridge into chorus, bridge into verse, or verse into bridge into chorus, casting director Dave Clemmons says: "I want a complete story, with no repeats, that shows off your voice in under a minute."[2]

4

Communicating What You Need

Quick question: Who is the most important person in your rock audition?

Not you, silly.

The accompanist.

Why, you ask? Because you need the accompanist to support you musically in a way that legit music doesn't require.

I've gone back and forth about where in the book this chapter goes. But here's the reason why it *needs* to be so early in the book: you have to be able to practice *all* of the things I'll be teaching you in this book, and in order to do that, the first thing you need to learn is *how* to get musical support so that no matter which accompanist you rehearse with (or how many different accompanists), you always get the same excellent results.

When you first start out, whether it's an audition for a theater season, summer stock, rep company, or even for a cruise ship, you will get a wide variety of legit musical theater accompanists. You may even get lucky and get someone who can wing it at playing rock.

When you get to the professional level of rock auditions, whether they are EPAs, ECCs, or open calls or appointments, you will most likely get someone who *can* play rock. But just because people *can* do it doesn't mean they are mind readers and will know how *you* need it to be done. So you need to learn how to communicate with your piano player so the two of you can give a rockin' performance together at your audition.

Here are some of the things I've heard accompanists say to actors during auditions.

"How do you want this to start?"

"How should I end this?"

"Are you going to tell me how this goes?"

"Look, honey, don't give me choices. I'm not good with multiple choices. Just tell me what you want."

Come on, pal. Is this the way you think your "big break" is going to happen? I'm asking because if I were a casting director and saw this interaction between you and your accompanist, I wouldn't want to hire you. Accompanists shouldn't have to ask you these questions.

Legit Versus Rock: Communication

Instructions for a legit musical theater song are very easy to communicate to an accompanist. You set the appropriate tempo, show any cuts, and you are ready to go. Audition accompanists on the most part know *every* legit musical song in existence, since they've played about 300 songs a day every day for years and years to make a living. If they're new to the business, or don't know the song well, it doesn't much matter, since the song was arranged to be sung in a musical.

Communicating instructions for a rock song asks for something radically different. Rock asks you to be in a *relationship* with the music.

When you sing legit music, you don't feel or hear the music when you perform. Seriously, you don't even know it is there. It is as if the musical accompaniment is a subconscious current carrying you through the action of your scene. The only time we ever consciously hear the music is when a scene takes place in a performance venue like a nightclub, such as at the Kit Kat Klub in the musical *Cabaret*. Then the singing of the song is a part of the plot, and the music is prominent.

With rock music, not only do you *know* that the music is there, you get the chance to express the rhythms, the changes, and the tempo with your body language and your voice. Feeling the presence of the music in your body is essential for success at a rock audition.

What a cool relationship. It may be the first healthy relationship you've ever had! The music will always be there for you. It'll never let you down. But you must treat the relationship with respect and care!

Your New Relationship

In the two minutes you have for this audition, I want you to pretend that you are in a scene with your piano player. The two of you are creating a special, musical experience together. Say you guys are friends . . . no, lovers. In order for *you* to be a great lover, you must take the initiative in communicating the feel and style of the song with a succinct clarity. By doing this, you empower them to do what they are there to do, which is to be a great scene partner. They will love you back in exactly the way that you want and deserve to be loved. They will play your music beautifully for you.

Adam Wachter, a professional musical director and one of the top accompanists for Broadway rock musical auditions, wants so desperately for actors to realize, "Your goal is to eliminate as many possible obstacles that will mess up your audition as you can—things that are under your control. People are petrified because they don't know what they are doing. They often put their audition book in front of me and basically say, 'Handle it. You are the rock player. You know what to do.' Well, that puts a lot of responsibility on me, someone they don't know, someone who doesn't care whether or not they get the job. I wouldn't go the extra mile for that person." [1]

You must also realize that not only is your accompanist a human being, but he is exhausted from sight reading *all day*. Accompanists are not usually acknowledged by actors as important, and it's a shame because they are busting their asses for us! That piano player could be a huge musical director and you don't even know it! So for god's sake, find out his name before you come in (there is usually a sign posted outside the door saying who is in the audition room), and then, after you enter, say, "Hello, Adam," for example, "How are you today?" And please listen for his answer. It's a wonderful opportunity for you to get yourself present and relax when you are terrified. We get so stuck up our own asses with fear that we don't even realize we have an opportunity to create this healthy relationship, even if its sixteen bars long.

Help Your Accompanist

Although it is not true of every accompanist, I'd say that when you meet most of them, they do not want you to shake their hand. It's perceived as inappropriate. Just say, "Hey there," and it'll be plenty. After you introduce yourself, you will say (with confidence), "Adam, do you know this tune? It's 'Let It Be' by Paul McCartney." Tell the accompanist the name of the song and who sang it.

Help him recall it by saying, "It goes a little something like this . . ." or "It goes . . . ."

Then take the accompanist directly to the *hook,* the catchiest part of the song, the part where at some point, somewhere—maybe at the laundromat or while driving in the car with *his* mother as a child—he heard this song playing on the radio. He'd rarely know the song from the verse; he'd *only* know it from this catchy part, which is usually the chorus. So take him there by singing that hook!

When you take him there, make sure to point to where the hook starts on the sheet music. Help the man out by giving him a visual.

Please heed my warning, as this is important. *Be careful* when you ask if the accompanist knows the song. You do not want to come across as condescending. You can phrase your question with trust in it. "Y'know this song?"

If the accompanist says no, then you can say, say, "cool!" and take him to the hook. It may remind him of the song or it may not, but at least he hears its essence.

If the song you intend to sing is obscure or very new, and you are positive that the accompanist *wouldn't* know it, I'd say something like, "This is 'Carbon Monoxide' by Regina Spektor. It goes like this . . ." and then take him to the hook, just like you would with a well-known song.

Please remember that the tone you use to communicate with him must be one of trust. Be kind. Be positive. Be clear and efficient. Have faith in the pianist. Especially if he doesn't play rock normally, your confidence and faith are imperative to his success . . . and his success leads to yours.

Adam Wachter says,

> If I say, "Yes, I know this song," that means I know the *original* version. I don't know your version. You have to tell me how you want *this* one to be. If you tell me clearly, that's what I'll do, as long as I have the chords. Oh. That's another thing. Don't get me started on the chords. When they photocopy the music, actors often chop off the chords at the top of the page or chop off the bass line on the bottom. But that's what we use, because we're rock players! Who do they think we are? We are reading the music off the page like you would read a monologue. If there's a line missing in the monologue, you can't just make it up! Neither can I with your music.[2]

Help your accompanist. Help him or her help you.

Translating the Feel

Meet Eddie Rabin. He's been playing Broadway rock auditions since I started in the business. Let me tell you something. This gentle, little man has a full *rock concert* in his hands. He is incredible. In his words, here's what Eddie wants you to understand about communicating successfully with an accompanist. "First of all, since our little 'rehearsal' may last only as long as five to ten seconds, I need you to be as succinct as possible in explaining your song to me. This applies to all kinds of music, of course, but especially for rock music, where the accompaniment can really tilt the balance. You should explain the tempo clearly, which means tapping out a beat while singing a non-ad lib part of your song."[3]

So after you've said the title of the song and who sang it, and you took the pianist to the hook, this is where you would indicate the tempo. When we give the tempo in a legit musical theater audition, we tap it with our foot and tap our thigh. But that alone will do Adam and Eddie little good. They also need to know what the song *feels* like.

When I sat in and observed the auditions for *Wonderland.* Eddie was on the keys, and I was very lucky to have been there. Why? Because no matter what song people gave him, he played it like he was playing with a full rock band. Someone gave him "Gravity" by Sara Bareilles and he played it the same way he would any other song you handed him: with vibrant, soulful rock energy.

"But 'Gravity' is a tender ballad," you might say.

That's right! But that girl didn't tell him it was a tender ballad. In fact, she didn't tell him anything. No one I saw audition that entire day bothered to translate what they wanted the songs to feel like to Eddie. Nobody. As a result, all day long I was looking at the startled faces of actors as they were realizing that the song didn't feel the same as when they sang along to it on the radio—and they didn't know why.

I'm so glad I'm here to help you guys.

Now let's talk about how to communicate or translate the elusive "feel." Eddie says, "Chances are good that I already know your song, as I've been playing rock for a *looonnnggg* time. Even so, you can really help me out by saying, 'You know, it's funk' or 'It's a little bossa nova-ish,' or something else to guide me to capture the feeling."[4]

A few other descriptive phrases you might use in a pop/rock audition are:

"It's a tender folk ballad."

"It's got a gospel feel."

"It's head-banging 1980s rock."

"It's old Motown."

"It's down and dirty blues."

"It's got a smooth R&B feel."

Telling the accompanist about the feel makes a huge difference. (Pencil the essence on the top left-hand corner of the sheet music, too.)

But guess what? With rock music, you have to *give* them the feel, too! Yes, tap your foot and tap your thigh with your hand, but communicate the essence of how the song feels with your *whole* body! Capture the feel of the song with your arms, your hips, your shoulders. If you're planning on rocking out, rock out with your whole body. Engage your entire body. Use body language. If the song is sexy, feel sexy when you tell the accompanist. If the song is gentle and tender, be tender in the way you translate the music to him. If you tell him, "It's head-banging 1980s rock," bang your head while you sing the hook so he gets the feel. If you do it for him, he will do it *with you* during your performance. Do it subtly, though. Save your performance for the actual audition.

Giving the feel of the hook to your "scene partner" brings him or her closer to the performance you hope to give. "My task is to put down a groove for you to settle into, and for you to float your vocal performance above it. That just seems to be the nature of rock music. The sooner we can lock into that groove, or 'feel,' the more successful our performance will be."[5]

Special note: The hints I am giving you here apply equally to R&B, gospel, country, and pop auditions—in other words, in any audition setting other than that of an audition for a standard Broadway musical.

You have *got* to work on this with the piano player before you audition with your song.

Special Tips on the Translation

Rock players love it when a singer knows the melody's relationship to the accompaniment. If you sing the melody *along* with some of the accompaniment to help give him the feel of the hook, then you are a rock star for sure. That song will be a satisfying meal for the creative team. Adam Wachter says, "What is *not* helpful is actors singing the melody out of tempo, like they are saying, 'You know this—da, da, da, da,' as they are rushing through it. The only thing most actors have been taught is not to snap their fingers at people when giving a tempo. As a result, they tend to speed through it. Then they don't give the feel correctly. Use the rhythms and the spaces *between* what you sing to give me the feel."[6]

Now, you are going to be a wreck because you are going to be *so* nervous. And your nerves are going to speed up your energy and speed up your tempo. You're going to feel like you don't want to be a burden to the creative team, and you're going to rush. Why do you "not want to take up any of their time"? You've waited *all day* for these two minutes!

Take.

Your.

Time.

When you give the tempo, what you need to do is watch for when the accompanist catches the feel. He will either say "Okay" or "Cool" or "I've got it." You'll know it. He also may "say" he's got it by picking up the rhythm you gave him with your body in *his* own body. Once he does get it, please, I beg of you, *stop* giving him the tempo! Why?

This is another moment where our terror tends to get the best of us. We start to doubt ourselves, and then we project our self-doubt on the piano player, and think, "Are you sure you've got it? Let me sing some more, just in case." If you didn't give too fast a tempo before, this is where you speed it up. It sabotages the performance, so that where we were fine for a moment, we are now . . . not fine.

Do everyone a favor. Put a recording of the artist singing the song or have someone lay down the accompaniment for you on your iPod or other MP3 player (use whichever version best reflects the tempo you need to do it in). Have a quick listen right *before* you go inside the audition room. Use this opportunity to get the feel of it and get the tempo tapping in your feet, so that you have it in your body, no matter how nervous you are. *This tip is a winner.*

Once you have the feel down perfect, all that's left is the roadmap. According to Eddie Rabin, a "roadmap" means the "repeats, intro (or lack thereof), and ending. If these things are clearly marked on your sheet music—and preferably highlighted—that's even better."[7]

The Roadmap

Adam Wachter prefers that actors go to the hook first, and then talk him through the layout. He says, "For the most part, the rock songs I play at auditions are not well laid out. It doesn't matter if it's a repeat-and-fade with eighty-five codas, four endings, and eight verses. Make it easy for me. Cut and paste the music in the way it needs to be sung."[8]

He continues, "That goes for the lyrics, too. It's the worst when the verse actors choose to sing is typed at the end of the song on the back page of the music. That makes it almost impossible for me to follow along with them. All you need to do is to white out the wrong words in the music and write in the ones you are planning to sing."[9]

After you give the accompanist the feel of the song in the hook, immediately show him anything special that he needs to be aware of in the sheet music. Take him right back to where the song starts and tell him *how* you want it to start, as well as what you need him to do for the ending. Highlight any special tempos, key changes, special introductions, and endings.

Since we have to create so many endings in rock music, please be super clear.

You could also take the accompanist to the hook, show him or her the cuts for the ending, and *then* show him or her how the song starts. This way would be just as valuable a roadmap. Anything is fine so long as the hook comes first!

Now, if the accompanist screws it up after all that instruction, and he plays it too fast or too slow, what do you do? Darling, even if it's not your fault, even if it's *his* fault, please say that it's yours! Stop the song and say something like, "Oh, I'm so sorry. I'm so excited to be here today that I gave you a very excited tempo! It's actually a little slower. My fault!" And then do it again and give him the appropriate tempo.

We must be responsible for ourselves. In real life, if something is *not* your fault, it's really *not* your fault. In the audition room, if it's *not* your fault, it *is* your fault. Being responsible mobilizes the situation. Being blaming doesn't. Just remember that you can make light of it.

It's the same thing when the tempo is too slow; you might say, "God, I feel so relaxed I gave you too slow a tempo. I'm so sorry. My fault!"

You don't need to say these specific things, but you get my point!

Then give the accompanist the proper tempo and start again.

When you are done with your audition, turn to the pianist and say, "Thank you. That was awesome." Because it will be.

Whispering at the Piano

Here's one last tidbit. It's about whispering at the piano.

Most actors I see audition whisper to the pianist. Why is that? What's the big secret? Unless the song contains a comedic surprise, there's really nothing to hide. In fact, it is actually better for you to be clear and present in the room when you give the pianist the feel of your song for the following reasons.

► They will see how well you communicate. A good communicator is hirable; a bad communicator is not.

► They'll also see how you treat the piano player. Considerate, humble people are hirable; arrogant, blaming people are not. Your etiquette in these situations is imperative.

► If the pianist just *cannot* play the song, if he destroys it, the casting team will know you did your best—you weren't the one who screwed it up.

When I asked Eddie Rabin if he had anything else he wanted to add, he said, "Don't bring in sheet music written expressly for the guitar. It's like a different language for us, which makes it cumbersome to decipher and navigate. I have done it, but it is a chore. It also comes across as inconsiderate toward the piano player. If you can't find the song in a piano version, see if you can pay someone to chart it for you."[10]

I am in full agreement with Eddie, and with Adam Wachter's definition of a successful rock audition. Adam says, "A successful pop/rock audition is one in which you've done the work. You've picked a great song, appropriate for show and era. The music is prepared; it's in the correct key, beautifully marked, wonderfully translated, and you know the feel. These basics are like building a foundation. You need your foundation, which is singing the song in the right way."[11] The sad thing is that people often don't even do the basics. If they did, then all they'd have to say as they arrive for their audition is, "Now I get to be a great performer."

You, the Singer

"The difference between rock music and musical theater is that rock music is 1 . . . 2 . . . 3 . . . 4 . . . and musicals are 5-6-7-8!"
—Elizabeth Ziff, band member of Betty

Help! I'm a legit soprano. I've never sung a rock song in my life! How on earth do I straight tone? And riffing? I don't know how to riff!"

Sure you do, darling.

I am going to demystify what the rock sound is so you can feel powerful, not petrified!

What Do Your Feelings Sound Like?

Screaming your notes, or "singing your face off" (also known in our community as "singing your face"), is not something I often encourage. Remember how, in the first chapter, we talked a bit about the pain of being "screamed at" all day long? And how dreadful that can be for the creative team?

How do *you* like being screamed at? When someone is screaming at you, is your heart open or do you shut down? Wouldn't you prefer to hear what someone is *feeling*?

Exactly which emotions are you connecting to when you are screaming, anyway? The only one I can think of is anger, and that is not an emotion. Screaming in anger is a reaction that you have to protect the emotion underneath it, which is hurt. It's selfish and belligerent, so it is not nearly as expressive as your hurt is. Wouldn't you *prefer* to express the colors and textures of an emotion that has the capacity to change, as opposed to feeling like you drove down a dead-end street? What if you were to not scream, but roar?

When we listen to the artists we love on the radio, we are affected by them because of the way their emotions travel on their voices. We hear the sound, and we are moved. I want you to affect the creative team with your voice. You have got to be vulnerable in order to be heard. You know this. You know this from your relationships in your real life, both the successful ones and the ones that break you apart. So take that beautiful sensitivity of yours, which is so valuable and necessary, and style your music with it.

Sometimes, all people can think about is hitting the high note. And you see people disconnect. Six bars before that high note, they leave their body. To watch how someone negotiates their voice to get to the high note, the *way* this climb happens, and the control they need to do it can be absolutely thrilling.

This is a pivotal moment in preparation for your rock audition. You have been impressed with the necessity of researching the music of different eras and shows. You've picked a song, arranged it, and figured out how to communicate the essence of your song with an accompanist. Now, we must get to work on vocal styling! The ability to style your music is what will set you apart from the hundreds of screaming banshees with whom you are going to be competing at your audition.

How does singing like you are living in the '50s sound different than if you are singing like you are living in the '80s? These decades were wildly different musically. You must learn to differentiate the specifics of each era's vocal demands and the dynamics within them so you can express these distinctions.

Meet my pal Tom Burke, a voice teacher I often work with in New York City (TomBurkeVoice.com). I feel confident in saying that Tom feels the same way I do when it comes to your voice. You must be dynamic! The reason why I brought him into the book is because I am not a voice teacher; I teach people how to "perform" songs. I direct and music direct sixteen- to thirty-two-bar cuts of songs. And so, I need him to describe in "voice teacher language" the things I teach people by example.

On the DVD that accompanies this book, I naturally demonstrate the sweetness, breathiness, nasality, emotional ache, straight toning, riffing, relaxed articulation, and glottal onsets that Tom describes in the next few pages. These are the tools you will need to create an authentic rock sound. So please be sure to watch those tracks when it is suggested.

Vocal Health and Versatility with Tom Burke: Incorporating Pop/Rock Styling into Your Musical Theater Training

Vocal Health

Transitioning from traditional musical theater singing to pop/rock singing may seem daunting. But perhaps surprisingly many key components of good technique remain the same no matter the genre in which you're singing. Here we'll explore where other genres converge with, and diverge from, pop/rock technique and show you how you are already on the right track. Regardless of the genre of your audition songs, all healthy singing requires the following components of my HMO plan.

Hydration: Your vocal folds need adequate hydration to move easily. The more hydrated you are, the less effort and breath you need to make sound. Avoid dehydration by minimizing caffeinated beverages and alcohol. If you are on any medications (for instance, inhalers, acne medications, anti-depressants), talk to your doctor about which of these may be harmful or dehydrating for your voice. To ensure optimal hydration, try steaming with a facial steamer twice a day for five minutes and drinking upwards of half your body weight in ounces of water.

Muscle tension management: Optimal alignment and total body strength are key components for all genres of singing, and especially high-powered rock singing. To get your body in top shape, I encourage you to be involved with some sort of bodywork tradition where you can learn the balance between healthy muscular work and excessive tension, improve your strength and stability, and maintain optimal alignment. I typically recommend exploring a combination of cardiovascular, resistance, and alignment training, such as weight training with a personal trainer or taking classes in yoga, Pilates, Feldenkrais, and Alexander technique.

Once you are involved with physical training, you will find that all great teachers essentially ask for the same things in terms of either your body or your voice. All singing styles require the following:

Feet shoulder-width apart

Grounding through the legs

Core strength

Natural curve in the spine (tailbone dropped—neither tucked under, nor hyper-extended)

Maximal width of the shoulders

Length through the cervical spine (neck)

Freedom in the ribs to allow for variations of the breath

Strength in the upper torso, especially in the *pectoralis major* (chest) and the *lattisimus dorsi* (back/shoulder blades) muscles

Open throat

High, soft palate in the mouth

Released tongue, lips, and jaw

Optimal lifestyle habits: Your voice is a reflection of your overall health. In order to deliver eight shows a week of high-powered rock singing in front of a large audience you need to be in optimal health. Consider mapping out your day to include the following:

Seven to eight hours of sleep

Consume a super-clean diet to facilitate stamina (also avoid foods that may exacerbate acid reflux, aka GERD)

Meditation

Short, frequent practice sessions to build up strength and avoid vocal burnout

Vocal Versatility: Continuums for Coolness

Having established proper vocal hygiene, you're now ready to learn techniques that will make you a versatile pop/rock singer. Some of these words will be foreign to you if you haven't studied in a musical conservatory, but in combination with watching Sheri perform these techniques on the DVD, and with a little practice on your own, they will make sense. We'll be discussing tonal onsets, registration, articulation, and vibrato variations.

Tonal onsets: The phrase "tonal onset" refers to the way we start making sound. In operatic singing, smooth onsets of singing are required. However, in pop/rock singing we try to emulate speaking. In real speech, we use a variety of onsets including *light glottal stops* (for example, "Oh man"), *glottal fry* (for example, a creaky door voice, achiness, or light gravel in your tired morning voice), and a variety of other effects that express emotion (for example, think of the long, breathy "H" sound in a flirty spoken onset, "Hhhey"). The word "glottal" refers to action of the epiglottis, the flap of skin in the back of your throat that must open when air moves through your vocal chords for sound to emerge.

Go through your repertoire of songs and pick out all the words that start with a vowel; then explore how many different ways you can begin these sounds. Notice the different emotional colors. Also, when you are listening to your playlists of music from different eras, listen to how some of your icons color the beginning of the words and plot them along this continuum:

Breathy onsets——Glottal fry——Smooth onsets——Glottal onsets

Registration: American pop and rock music is a huge category that spans decades! It is impossible to come up with a specific recipe for all the variations. But all pop/rock music shares a connection to the speaking voice, or a sense that the singer is "speaking in the key" (that means singing it like you would speak it). In training for musical theater and opera, you may have learned specific techniques to manage your chest, mix, head, and belt voices. Sometimes knowing about these techniques can make us feel as if singing and speaking are wildly different. But imagine if singing and speaking emerge from just *one* voice without any separation. As we strive for connection to the authentic speaking voice, what does it feel like to speak in the key?

You want to wake up your ears to sounds that may not have been part of your original vocal training. Instead of limiting yourself to thoughts of chest–mix–head, let your ears and voice explore a more spoken-based continuum, such as whisper–quiet talking–conversation–call–shout. Also listen to how pop/rock uses many operatic and traditional musical theater "no-nos," such as breathiness, nasality, and other so-called bright sounds that come from having a larynx oriented in a more mid or mid-high position vs. a low, operatic position.

Watch YouTube videos of various tongue and mouth positions. Search keywords, such as "vocal training" and "voice technique," and you'll find videos on numerous aspects of voice training.

Experiment with different tongue positions and vowels on the melody (using an "Ahhh" sound) to see which ones bring out, first, your authentic pop/sound and, second, the best sound for a particular decade. By this I mean, sing in on an "Ee" vowel vs. an "Eh" vowel and notice which one sounds more like pop music. Each of these sounds can be safe and beautiful provided that you maintain the key components of vocal health listed above.

Have fun and play with your voice along this continuum:

Whispered voice—Quiet talking—Conversation—Call—Shout

Articulation: Articulation refers to the process of producing consonants and vowels. Rules for articulation again will vary with the genre and decade, so be prepared to play with a wide variety of articulation techniques. Think of two different continuums:

Mainly vowels—Mainly consonants
Slurred speech—Over-articulated speech

Go through your song repertoire and audio libraries. As you play and listen to the masters of rock, where would you plot them along the preceding continuums? When the casting director or musical director of the show for which you are auditioning asks you for more or less of a certain quality of your voice, get to know how to dial up or dial down your articulation to suit the style.

Vibrato variations: By now, I'm sure you see a pattern emerging with me: no hard answers! Even with vibrato, there are wild variations, some guidelines, but no rules. You really have to listen to how vibrato can vary in style from decade to decade and by individual singer. I can tell you that there is definitely less vibrato in rock than in the world of opera, but after saying that, the conversation becomes tricky. It's easier to think of our continuums, or options, again, where you have:

Total straight tone—Total vibrato

Or think of placing vibrato in the:

Beginning of phrase—Middle of phrase/verb—End of phrase

"The Cry" vs. "The Throw Away"

Finally another subtle but important stylistic variation is what I call "the cry" vs. "the throw away." In musical theater, we often speak the body of the lyric, perhaps emphasize the verbs, then sing or cry on the ends of phrases, perhaps with a little vibrato. If you listen to many pop singers, they will often have "cry" at the beginning of the phrases and then "throw away," mumble, deemphasize, or speak the ends of phrases. This differentiation is huge for singers who are transitioning from traditional musical theater singing to pop/rock styling.

Listen to how country music differs from Top 40 country, and to how 1980s pop vibrato is different than what you hear in the contemporary pop music played on the radio today. If you know the era of your song and the era of the musical for which you are auditioning, insights about the vocal styling used in different periods can be crafted into the way you do your audition song.

Gosh, there is way more to talk about, but here comes Sheri again.

A Quick Caution

Tom Burke is correct that vocal health and vocal versatility are closely related. A voice can be damaged by singing a hard rocking song much more easily than by singing one of Nellie Forbush's songs from *South Pacific*. An authentic rock sound is either a gift you've naturally been given or it's something you train to achieve. Nonetheless, many people audition thinking, "I'm just going to go for it!," and then they push their voices too hard and pay a steep price for it.

You have to understand that the vocal acrobatics that make rock songs on the radio *seem* like they would be great audition pieces were produced in a recording studio. You are therefore trying to emulate effects that are unnatural with your natural voice. These songs are treated, mixed, and mastered by engineers. They are sung in a microphone. Let's also not forget the magic of "auto tune," a music program on the computer that can actually *tune* an out-of-tune singer's voice!

Don't put yourself in a situation where you have to sing a rock song until you know how to do it in a healthy way. Pushing beyond your current level of training and versatility is not going to get you a job, and the professionals understand that it might damage your voice. They need to hear a voice that can do that eight times a week. I've been at auditions where after the singer leaves the room, the creative team will comment, "They can't get through three shows, never mind eight shows *a week*."

That caution being duly noted, let's review some details about the technical specifics of each rock era.

Style and Time Period Technical Specifics

In Chapter 2, we discussed different styles and time periods in rock history. We know that every decade was different, and that the people of each decade had different needs. When learning to create an authentic rock sound pertaining to a given time period, it is important to study the performances of rock singers who were popular then.

Do you remember my suggestion to set up different stations on Pandora.com in order to look for song material? As you listen to those stations you will learn about many singers you never heard of before and learn many amazing songs that are unfamiliar to you. Perhaps the biggest gift of Pandora, however, is the opportunity it provides to study different ways people expressed themselves musically in a variety of time periods.

Ask yourselves these questions on elements of their vocal styling:

▶ How did they phrase music in this era? A musical phrase is similar to a spoken phrase. How do people say things?

▶ Is there an emotional ache in their voices? The "ache," is the sound of a singer's need. How does the singer allow the emotion to color the phrasing?

▶ How did people riff in this era? Technically a riff is a short musical phrase, a run of notes, and often a riff is a repeating phrase.

▶ When do people choose to straight tone? When do they use vibrato? Straight toning is a simple tone without vibration. Vibrato is a pulsing tone that can be faster or slower depending on the singer.

▶ When are their songs breathy?

After hearing music of the day, you can form educated opinions about how and why people sang the way they did. To me, that's the best way to study how to style music.

Earlier in the book we talked about the styles of the different time periods. Please go back to Chapter 2, and give it a once-over to remind yourself of the differences between the cultures of the eras. Get in the habit of being informed. We talked about what people were like. We talked about what was happening in the world, and why people were the way they are, what influenced them to write the music they did, and how music influenced humanity as it did. But what does this mean for us as singers?

Let's talk time periods again, shall we?

Rock Technique of the 1950s and 1960s

The music was as crisp and clean as the clothes and how people presented themselves. The music was easy. It was light and formulaic. It was harmonic. Even when people were singing about losing the one they loved, the music was still light-hearted, with a strong rhythm. The girls and the boys had backup singers who danced. We saw groups like Martha and the Vandellas, Gladys Knight and the Pips, the Four Tops, the Spinners, and Diana Ross and the Supremes. The music was not indulgent, and singers—even if they were great soul singers—still stayed in the structure with incredible ease. Their voices were precise. The music was precise. As a result, there was little room for vibrato. In fact, the songs of this era are those for which I believe speaking in the key will serve you well.

I'd like to talk about riffing some more, specifically in this time period. The riffs here are quick. I'm going to compare them to the song styling of Christina Aguilera right now, even though we'll *really* talk about her later. That girl is riff-tastic. She's freakin' amazing at it. She really is. But most of what she does, I'd say, is more of a wild vocal impulse as opposed to, say, emotional specifics; she's really doing it because she can. Please understand, people didn't do things relentlessly because they *could* back in the '50s and '60s. That's a newer, more contemporary style. They did something musically back then only because they were emotionally moved to do it. And since times were simpler, the emotions that created riffs were simpler, and therefore the riffs were relatively simple. So just know, if you're going to riff in a '50s or '60s tune, less is more.

The time has come for you to experience your first taste of what this looks and sounds like in action. The DVD inside the back cover of the book contains the video tracks demonstrating vocal, physical, and interpretive techniques that lead to well-rounded audition performances. You will begin by inserting the DVD in your computer and going to "Voice Intro." Click on the "'50s and '60s." As I am demonstrating I want you to notice the details and nuances of how I make these sounds. Watch it as many times as you need to, and feel free to do it along with me. Be attentive and you'll pick this up quickly!

Rock Technique of the 1970s

Darling, remember when we talked about the '70s? The Vietnam War had taken many lives. Youth were rebelling. They were raw, emotional, and all of a sudden it was necessary to explore life. So rock music became deeper, grittier, and more poetic. We lost the necessity for the stability of a steady rhythm. The music got darker and performers' voices were richer, earthier, more grounded.

Have a listen to Janis Joplin, Jimi Hendrix, and Heart's first few albums. See how down and dirty we were getting. Look at the great folk movement as it was represented by Joni Mitchell; Bob Dylan; Joan Baez; Peter, Paul and Mary; and the Mamas and the Papas, and see that we went from being straightforward in our music to being poetic.

Voices reflected the time, and so they were extended. People were holding out their notes longer, the sound was no longer crisp and clean; instead it was messy, raw, dangerous, emotional, gritty, gravelly, and—when singers were interpreting poetry—the sound was mindful, contemplative, and fluttery. People were singing as if they were reading poetry out loud. It was sort of like jazz. They knew the structure of the music, and they interpreted the music inside the structure. So we can say that the music of the '70s is free, the voices are dynamic and emotional, and singers were starting to play with dynamics. Some moments were quiet, some moments soared. And they were exploring everywhere in between.

Rock critic Terry Bloomfield writes, "The authentic came to be seen not just as the genuine, that is some kind of 'real' 'folk' art, but also as raw, direct emotion that would somehow break through the 'trappings of showbiz.' In the hands of the counterculture, authenticity 'swelled up to embrace emotional honesty and sincerity, autobiographical truth and political correctness."[1]

Folk music must never be belted. It must not, must not, must not. I was at an audition, and someone sang a Bob Dylan song and screamed it at us.

Bob Dylan was a peaceful protestor, darling friend. Peaceful. Click on "'70s."

Pop Technique of the 1980s

There's a lot to tell you about the vocals of '80s pop music. First of all, there was tons of straight toning. It would sound dreadfully wrong, therefore, if you put vibrato all over this stuff. The singers of the day were Cyndi Lauper, Madonna, Annie Lenox, and Pat Benatar. How much vibrato did they have in their voices? Little to none. The sound was clean again, like the sound of the '60s. The music was clean and synthesized, so it was no longer raw. The intended emotions were simple and light.

Rock Technique of the 1980s

Well, this is a similar notion to the pop technique of the same era. If you are singing Journey, Styx, and Foreigner, be mindful that they were straight toning the crap out of their music. There are no fluttery, floating, poetic riffs in their vocal styling.

Click on "'80s."

Contemporary Rock Music Styling

Contemporary rock music covers so many bases. My God! If we look at some of the leaders in rock music, artists like Kurt Cobain, Kelly Clarkson, Alanis Morissette, No Doubt, 4 Non Blondes, and

Daughtry, we find that the sound is raw once again. If you are supposed to be brooding and emotional, the sound *must* reflect that. So if the pain is deep, what's the sound? It is raw.

Click on "Contemporary Rock."

Contemporary Pop Music Styling

Here is where I will lovingly bring Christina Aguilera back into our conversation. She is joined in the genre of contemporary pop by singers like Beyoncé, Miley Cyrus, Justin Timberlake, and Britney Spears, artists who all have one thing in common: their music is highly produced (meaning the producers mix it in the studio until it is *just so*). These artists also use lots and lots of vocal dynamics. Their songs are therefore a great place to riff, sweet pea.

And please know that even though I still believe you should never riff senselessly, you still would consider *this* the place to show off your vocal prowess. If you are putting a comedic spin on it, then yes, riff yourself senseless! Make fun of how ruthlessly these singers riff and their riff fests.

A very exciting article from the *New York Times* showed up in my hands while I was editing the book, and its timing was impeccable. The title of the article, written by David Browne, is "Trilling Songbirds Clip Their Wings." In this article, he discusses *melisma*, which "in its simplest form is a vocal technique in which a series of notes is stretched into one syllable." This is what we are referring to when we talk about "melismatics" like Christina Aguilera, Mariah Carey, Jennifer Hudson, Beyoncé, and male performers like Brian McKnight and Tyrese, and their ability to riff beyond our wildest dreams. What this article mentions, however, is that the trend is moving from this sound to a straighter tone, and you can find it in singers like Lady Gaga, whose onstage dramatics do what these singers have been doing vocally. Even Pink, who started out more as a pop/hip-hop/R&B singer, is now more conventional with her hot pop tunes. Browne writes, about Katy Perry, "Ms. Perry opts for short breathy gulps in her singing. Her voice occasionally glides into an upper register, but it mostly aims to convey likability and approachability, not prowess and imperiousness." He adds, "melisma may have run its cultural course," and concludes, "pop's new divas may not be able to ascend to vocal heights the way Ms. Aguilera still can in 'Burlesque.' But in many ways, they're better suited for the post-crash economy. Every so often even pop music has to downsize."

What does this mean to you as a singer? Get with the program! Click on "Contemporary Pop."

Developing Musicianship

By using Tom Burke's techniques, along with studying the way artists express themselves on your Pandora stations, you will be able to develop the specific dynamics of the vocal styles easily and gain an understanding of what it's like to be in a relationship with this music. You can apply these techniques to any genre of rock musicals *and* create a sound that is flavorful, dynamic, and, ultimately, authentic—and always healthy.

More than just learning to style a song in order to book a rock musical, I insist that you become a great musician. Not only will it help you become more successful, you also will be an incredibly dynamic artist and human being if you do. To guide you, I spoke to some of the great sages in the musical theater community on the subject of developing one's musicianship. The first was Tom Kitt, a classically trained pianist. At twelve or thirteen he discovered Billy Joel, Elton John, Paul McCartney, and Bruce Hornsby. In high school, he developed a love of jazz. It wasn't until college that he studied musical theater, at which point he dove into Cole Porter, Richard Rodgers, and Stephen Sondheim.

> *Tom:* If you look at *Next to Normal,* the opening number, "Just Another Day," is in a folk rock style. The next song, "Everything Else," is in a classical style. "My Psychopharmacologist and I" follows and is a combination of theatrical and jazz styles, followed by "Perfect for You," which uses a mixture of folk rock and impressionistic romantic styles. "I Miss the Mountains" returns to folk/pop, and later, "Didn't I See This Movie" is straightforward rock and roll. I wanted to tell this emotional story by using the rock idiom, but I did not want to define everything by it. The musical tone must be led by the dramatic moment and not the other way around. In order to do this effectively, I think it helps to have a wide knowledge of many styles. Having them at your disposal allows you to create dynamic story-driven music that can shift in tone and contour, allowing for a deeply emotional and varied experience.[2]

And this philosophy won Tom a Tony Award for Best Original Score for the absolutely stunning and outrageous musical *Next to Normal* in 2009. Co-written by Brian Yorkey, *Next to Normal* was also awarded a Pulitzer Prize in 2010. This show is a perfect example of hearing his musical influences on his songwriting.

Tom: It gives you the greatest palate possible. Part of what makes you excel in one particular area is a wide knowledge covering many different areas. For instance, my classical background helped immensely in creating the string parts for the punk musical *American Idiot.* And this pursuit of knowledge and wide-ranging musicality should not be limited to writing, but can be found in performance as well. For auditions, I look for the singer's interpretation of a song to tell me who they are, and how the song makes them feel. I am as affected by someone breaking my heart singing the song "River" by Joni Mitchell as I am by someone belting to the rafters.[3]

I *had* to ask Alex Lacamoire, the music director of *In the Heights, High Fidelity*, and *Bat Boy,* about music, knowing that on top of these great shows, he also arranged the music for *9 to 5, Legally Blonde,* and *Wicked.* I interviewed him when he was serving as music director for the original production *Bring It On,* which has Tom Kitt as one of its composers. When I asked Alex how someone learns to be a great rock singer, he said, "The best training is to listen. Listen to the radio and check out how people phrase the melody. Listen to all the different styles. They're only going to influence your performance. Theater, rock, R&B, and pop, learn them all. Researching these styles is going to influence everything that you do, so you will have a performance that is dynamic and flavorful. Cross-pollinating is your best bet."[4]

The reason why we need to "cross-pollinate" ourselves by listening to different genres of music is that, for example, rock songs can have a gospel feel. Similarly, folk songs can be infused with R&B. Pop could have a disco feel. Rock could have an R&B feel. Country can be pop, blues, or gospel. Folk can have a country feel, a blues feel, or a pop feel. Or a song could be rock, blues, and R&B all at once. Remember we spoke about all of this in Chapter 3?

Each style of music can be used as a different tool. Understanding this is what makes a singer *a great musician.* Having access to any style in any moment potentially makes your song richer and more delicious. Personally, my musical influences are Aretha Franklin, Laura Nyro, George Michael, Michael Jackson, Stevie Wonder, Pink, Tori Amos, Joni Mitchell, Etta James, Lauryn Hill, Elton John, Meatloaf, Janis Joplin, Kenny Loggins, Kate Bush, India Arie, Jill Scott, Chaka Khan, Whitney Houston, Rufus Wainwright, Patti LaBelle, Led Zeppelin, Nick Drake, Bette Midler, Richie Havens, Barbra Streisand, Patty Griffin, Dusty Springfield, Gladys Knight, and Joe Cocker. You can hear their influence on me when I sing!

I spoke with Stephen Oremus—the original music director and current music supervisor of *Wicked,* music director of *9 to 5,* music supervisor for *Avenue Q* and *All Shook Up*—while he was working as the music director for both the productions of *Tales of the City* and *The Book of Mormon* (upcoming at the time of this writing). He also arranged the music for *all* of these shows!

Here's what Stephen had to say:

> Musically speaking, there are so many different styles that are required by people in *Wicked* because our whole concept is a bunch of different musical hybrids. It was about creating a very rich, textured musical world. The ensemble has a very difficult task because they are required to a sing a wide variety of styles, from more traditional legit operatic singing to traditional Broadway to a pop sound.
>
> We never cast people that can do just one thing. Everyone is really required to have a wide range of styles. While every show is different, more often than not modern musical theater is incorporating a wider array of different vocal styles. As a music director of any show, you want people that have really great control vocally and the ability to execute a variety of styles. That's my palette, as a vocal arranger. It's a *super* crucial thing for any performer to have as much vocal versatility as possible.[5]

Are you guys catching my drift? These outrageous musical directors and composers are all telling you that they want a flavorful, contoured, expressive, and versatile performance from you. So give it to them!

A Deeper Relationship

Once you allow yourself to be influenced by all these different styles, you then get to look at the bigger picture. It is not just about your voice; it's about the music.

Michael McElroy has some very juicy advice for you! He says,

> I need to hear your understanding of the music. I need to hear your musicianship, the *musician* in your voice. Not just the singer, but the musician. There is a difference between being a singer and a musician. A musician understands the music, the whole song—not just the part *you* sing. That's not the song. You *must* study sight reading and ear training. You have to be a great sight reader. You have to access your emotions in the music—quickly. Don't let your lack of understanding of music get in your way. The musical theater art form deserves our respect.[6]

So when you turn on your iPod or MP3 player to listen to your music, lie down on your bed and really listen to it. Listen for the drums. Listen to the bass line. Are there any string instruments? What's *their* melody? A horn? Backup singers? What is the music telling you about how your melody needs to be in relationship with it?

More goodies from Alex Lacamoire:

> I am caring less and less about a singer's range, and I'm caring more and more about their sound. I want to know that whatever you sing, you can sing it with passion or joy or heartbreak or whatever the moment requires. If you can hit the "money note" at the end of a song and sustain it for eight bars, then cool. But the high notes? That's approximately 25 percent of the package that I'm seeking. I also want to hear the rhythm in your voice. I want to see how you keep time. I like to see if you're "inside the grid" rhythmically. I want to feel if you are hitting the off-beats and bouncing against the beat. Can you feel the pulse? I want to know if you can groove. I want to know if you can be in the pocket of this music.[7]

See?! He wants you in the pocket!

If being in the pocket means being inside the music, what does "backphrasing" mean? This term is commonly used in contemporary pop/rock music, so you need to know it. If the music is steady and you are right behind it, this is called back phrasing. The name really suits itself. Your phrasing is back behind the music. It is relaxing into it; it's feeling your voice being pulled forward by the accompaniment.

Note: When you choose to back phrase, make sure to tell your accompanist to "keep a slow and steady 4", and say, "I'll follow you." *I* will follow *you!* If you are back phrasing, you *are* following them, so they *need* to keep it steady for you. And you need ot kindly tell them that.

Click on "Backphrasing."

Vocal Styling Is Just the Beginning

From this chapter, you've learned that your audience needs to hear you be emotionally expressive. "Having a great singing voice" is a fine thing, but it is more important how you use your voice to express your emotions, as this has the potential to rock the creative team's world in an audition. In the next chapter, we'll look at how to tap into your emotions to give them the dynamic and versatile sound they are seeking.

You and Your Feelings

"Perfumes are the feelings of flowers."
—Heinrich Heine, *The Hartz Journey*

What we know about any song you choose to sing in an audition is that your feelings are so strong that you can no longer speak. In this moment, you *must* sing. With a rock song, the reason you are singing has everything to do with the story that *you* have created.

Remember, a rock song is not a piece of a bigger story, like a song from a legit musical would be; it doesn't move a plot along. It is an act of self-expression. Therefore, you have permission and are being requested—even expected—to interpret your rock song in a simple, inventive, deep, clever, poetic, real, authentic, sensitive, funny, fun, wild, and creative way. Based on *you*.

This is your chance to show people who you really are.

I like to consider the rock musical community the Island of Misfit Toys. Are you familiar with the old classic, stop-motion animation Christmas special *Rudolph the Red-nosed Reindeer*? Burl Ives played the voice of the narrator. It first aired on television in 1964 and has been on TV at Christmas ever since. Rudolph, who is considered different because he has a big red nose that lights up all the time, runs away from Santa Claus (with an elf who wants to be a dentist) and is welcomed to the island by a jack-in-the-box puppet named Charlie, a spotted stuffed elephant, a choo-choo train with square wheels on its caboose, a water pistol that shoots jelly, a bird that doesn't fly (it swims), a cowboy that rides an ostrich, and a boat that can't float.[1]

That's us, you guys. We became performers because we wanted to be loved and accepted for our unique presence in the world. We use our art to express our feelings about ourselves. But we often feel as if the "little boys and girls" don't want us 'cause we are "unconventional," so we are left to wrestle with the fear of being rejected and often end up isolating ourselves. I hear from a lot of my students that when they were studying acting in college they fell through the cracks because they didn't fit into a "type" like an ingénue or a leading man. Eventually, they were put into the category called "quirky," which left them with nowhere to go to embrace or celebrate their uniqueness. It was as if their individuality was inappropriate for musical theater.

Being a "misfit toy" is a gift, not a curse! It means you are special. Rock songs *insist* on your individuality. This is great news because there is no character that you "have to play" to audition for a rock musical. *You* are the character. You only have to be *you* in every way possible. The way the creatives get to know how you perform is by seeing you connect to your story. Connecting to your story is how you get called back, and getting called back is how you get a job.

Don't give the people behind the table what you think they want. Instead, show them the "you" you really are. You are *allowed* to share your feelings. No one is stopping you. In fact, the people behind the table *pray* for you to do it.

I must have spoken with at least five people who mentioned that Sutton Foster played herself when she auditioned for the Broadway production of *Thoroughly Modern Millie*. Although she was not the original pick for the lead, her story is remarkable because she was plucked from the chorus at the last minute to assume the leading role prior to the show's opening. She then went on to win the 2002 Tony Award for Best Leading Actress in a Musical, gaining stardom.[2] Isn't that awesome? Just from being herself. And why would you say no to being yourself? Being yourself is liberating, creative, fun, satisfying, healing, and grounding.

Dare to Tell an Emotional Story

I'm going to teach you how to create an emotional story with a rock song. Instead of thinking you are auditioning for a musical, begin with allowing yourself to wonder, "If I was alone in my room right now and no one was looking, what would I be going through as I said these words?" You must capture this kind of intimate moment in your song and create an arc with it that is dramatic, even if it's emotionally subtle.

I don't want you to abandon your musical theater training and replace it with what I'm teaching you. But I want you to have both techniques at your fingertips. In fact, *I dare you* to incorporate this technique for emotional storytelling into your legit auditions.

Ready?

When you listen to a rock song on the radio, it evokes emotions in you, right? You feel your broken heart. A song may lift you out of a crappy place. Or perhaps a song reminds you of an earlier time of your life. It identifies feelings that you have but to which you've never put a name.

Does a song on the radio make you want to get up and shake your ass? Or does it make you want to throw yourself on the ground and weep like a little kid having a tantrum in the middle of the mall? If it moves you at all, this means you are connecting to it and letting it affect you. This emotional relationship with the music is the key to storytelling in your rock audition.

What if, when you were singing, instead of telling the story of the song, you connected to the feelings that the song actually evokes in you?

The coolest thing happened to me in one of my classes. My student Justin Gentry saw another student, Stephanie Fittro, perform her song on the last day of class, and he told her: "When you sang that song, I understood what the artist was feeling when he wrote it." This was a proud moment in my teaching career. Stephanie was interpreting the material based on how the song related to her life. And *that*, my friend, is what acting a rock song is about!

Let's use "Let It Be," one of the songs we arranged into an audition-sized cut in Chapter 4 as an example. When I hear Paul McCartney sing "Let It Be," as an interpreter of rock music, I think, "Oh my God, I do not know how to let myself be. I need to let myself heal." Other times, I think globally as I listen: "We need to be kinder to each other so that we can let this planet heal." McCartney's singing evokes emotions in me about my life, life in general, and my need for peace. It does so because the *essence* of "Let It Be" is peace.

The reason why this song evokes these emotions in me isn't because McCartney was "acting the song" when he recorded it. He was *feeling* it. He was very clear about how he felt. And in his expressing how *he* felt, he allowed me to connect to how *I* feel.

The problem you face when you're on an audition, though, is that you're not in the car blasting tunes on the radio. An audition is not a rock concert. It is an opportunity to book a part in a musical. Therefore, you absolutely *must* engage your audience in a dramatic way. As Gayle Seay from Wojcik-Seay Casting says, "I don't care what your voice sounds like. But don't you dare not tell a story. Just singing is not theater. You are auditioning for a musical."[3]

When you go to prepare your emotional storyline, ask yourself these essential questions:

► What is the artist saying about himself/herself in this song?
► What is the essence of the song?
► What is the song's message?

Answering these questions does not mean I want you to figure out "what the story is about." You don't need to do that. We already know what the story is . . . it's in the lyrics. What I mean is you need to understand what the artist is *feeling* during this song. In singing a rock song, a journey must be taken through the emotions that are underlying the lyrics. As a performer you can make a roadmap of emotions to follow through the storyline that you invented when you cut your song into a *musical* roadmap (as in Chapter 5). But first you have to name your emotions.

One of the best classes I've ever taken was called Rasaboxes, which was taught by an extraordinary resident teacher at Ithaca College named Paula Murray Cole. She teaches the concept (originated by Richard Schechner in the 1980s and 1990s) to actors all over the world. I took her class in New York City, and my mind was officially blown. The class description says it teaches the participant how to become an "Athlete of the Emotions." Recently, I phoned Paula to discuss the subject of auditions.

"Paula," I began, "when I ask people how they feel about the story they are telling, their answer is often really general. My students come to me not knowing who they are or how they feel, and so their auditions are dull and lifeless. An actor will leave the audition room feeling like, 'Well, I guess that was fine,' and a casting person by contrast will say, 'That actor seemed nice, but I have no idea who this person is.' And then the actor's headshot and résumé get put into the 'no' pile."

Paula replied, "Well, we are told that having, working with, or playing with your feelings is indulgent, isolating, and self-serving. So people shy away from their feelings, and it hurts us. All of us. It closes the door to a range of expressivity that needs exploration, because it makes you a facile performer."[4]

Do you understand what she means by facile? In the theater, facile means being adjustable, pliable, bendable, and flexible.

Let me tell you a little bit about my experience with Paula and the rasaboxes, a contemporary training technique designed to help us dig deeper into our experience and expression of our emotions.

The Sanskrit word "rasa" can be translated as "juiciness, taste, flavor, or essence." How delicious! In Indian culture, rasa is used to describe a number of different elements or experiences. Rasas are the various flavors in food (such as salty, bitter, sweet, pungent, astringent, and sour)[5] or *emotional* "flavors" that can be "tasted" in a performance. According to an ancient Indian treatise on performance, *The Natya Shastra,* there are eight different rasas, [6] as follows:

Wonder (*adbhuta*)

Love (*sringara*)

Fear/shame (*bhayanaka*)

Disgust/revulsion (*bibhatsa*)

Courage (*vira*)

Laughter (*hasya*)

Sadness/compassion (*karuna*)

Rage (*raudra*)

During the class, we drew eight boxes on the floor to represent the emotional rasas and, using chalk, we colored the boxes with what we thought each rasa felt like. Then we would step into a rasabox and see what it felt like to *enter into the feeling*, and be *inside* of it. We were to form no opinions, judgments, or thoughts about it, but to *just feel* its essence. I asked Paula how this exercise could be translated to the rock audition experience. Here are some tidbits of our longer conversation.

Paula: Let's use one rasa, for example, *adbhuta* (wonder, marvel). What is the sensation for you when you see something fabulous? What is the energy of this? What happens to you when you are standing on the edge of a cliff? The breathing halts and everything becomes fascinating. What if adbhuta is in your eyes, your face? What if it's in your knees? It's letting this sensational energy form, and then letting your emotional experience come from that invitation. The invitation is to connect to your feelings through breath, voice, body, and sensation.

Sheri: So you're saying that this isn't a thinking thing. It's a connecting-to-your-feelings thing. If I asked my students how a song makes them feel, and they say, "It makes me upset," you would say to them . . . ?

Paula: Well, let's detail that. What kind of upset is it? Is it rage? Or is it sadness and compassion? Is it distaste, disgust? Or is it fear? What does fear feel like to *you?* Where and how are you sensing this in your body, breath, voice, imagination? Sadness is a very different experience in the body and the voice than rage is. It's not just upset. "Upset" is general.

What Paula is saying is that rasas are not emotions. They are the *juiciness* of your emotions. Why be general when your feelings are so juicy!

This is scary, huh? Having all this room and freedom to have your emotions? A little overwhelming, even? If you think so, you're not alone. Most actors don't know what to do when they're given control. We are so used to being told what to do. Do you remember the conversation I had with the casting team at the Roundabout Theatre

Company in Chapter 1? Go reread their comments. Stephen Kopel of Roundabout said, "Freedom is why people crash and burn."

If you find that having the freedom to feel and create your own storyline is overwhelming, don't worry, sweet cheeks. I've got the solution. In the immortal words of the great Julie Andrews, "Structure gives you the freedom to fly."

Here's the structure that's going to put you in control of your audition experience. We are going to treat your song like a road trip . . . and *you* are our designated driver.

Name Your Destinations

On the road trip we'll call "your song," you are going to make a few emotional "pit stops." Therefore you need to map out *where* those pit stops will be along the way. Since you are the driver, you get to take us wherever you want. So you'd better take us to see some amazing sights!

Before I go any further, your song, like any piece of art, could be interpreted in many different ways. What I am about to show you is my interpretation of a song. I am basing this interpretation on *my* life experiences. *Your* version will be totally different than mine, and both will work if they are true.

Let's start with the lyrics. Always start with the lyrics—in this case the words to "Let It Be."

When I find myself in times of trouble
Mother Mary comes to me
Speaking words of wisdom, let it be

When I look at the first set of lyrics, what I feel as a human being comes from the "clues" that the lyrics give me. I am in trouble, and when I am in trouble, the feeling I feel is fear.

The emotion that is my first pit stop in this song is fear.

And in my hour of darkness
She is standing right in front of me
Speaking words of wisdom, let it be

I am in such a heightened state of fear that a benevolent apparition, a spiritual guide, comes to me. So now I am in awe, and I wonder if this is really happening.

The emotion that is my second pit stop is wonder.

Let it be, let it be/Let it be, let it be
Whisper words of wisdom/Let it be

As I hear Mother Mary giving me these words of wisdom, the first thing I feel is shame about needing the help and not being able to handle this situation on my own.

The emotion that is my third pit stop is shame.

Let it be, let it be/Let it be, let it be

When I repeat the chorus, I hear what she is saying to me, which is that it's okay to ask for help, that asking for help makes me a strong woman. And hearing these words, I feel what it would be like to have compassion for myself simply because I am human.

The emotion in the fourth pit stop is compassion.

Whisper words of wisdom/Let it be

Finally, I thank my spirit guide for coming to me in this time of need and letting me know that everything is going to be okay.

The final emotion on this road trip is gratitude/grace.

These feelings are your destinations, your pit stops. These pit stops are your rasas, but you are not limited to expressing the eight emotions in the rasaboxes that Paula taught me. Again, rasas are not emotions; rather, they are the *flavors* of your emotions. So the possibilities for emotional expression in any song are truly limitless. Any emotion that is real, true, and full will do!

Create Your Roadmap

In 2001, I created a show called *Soulstice* for which I took a bunch of songs off the radio, arranged them, and strategically placed them in an order that created a self-fulfilling prophecy. It's amazing that a project I did ten years ago would end up being not only what I do for a living, but would also become a diagram in a book about my work as well. Life is so cool. Here is what the diagram of "Let It Be" looks like. You'll see five emotional destinations in the circles I've drawn, which correspond with the emotions in the parentheses below the interpretation of the lyrics in the section above (fear, wonder, shame, compassion, and gratitude/grace).

There may be fewer (or more) pit stops in a song depending on the song. If you are auditioning for a musical with a sixteen-bar cut, it doesn't mean there are less pit stops than in a thirty-two-bar cut. These together form the structure of your "emotional subtext."

This is where the details of *your* personal story come into play.

As a rule when you are singing rock music, you must *feel* the emotions of the text. If you say the word "sweet," feel the sweetness. I consider this approach *very* similar to the way to act Shakespeare. The

"Let It Be"

language of a rock song, like Shakespeare's language, allows you to savor your feelings. So in this story, you wouldn't *show* me your fear or your shame, you would *feel* your fear. You would *feel* your shame.

When students first come to me, the simplicity of this approach scares the crap out of them. They feel like they are not acting. They are afraid they are "emotionally masturbating" because they aren't "playing a scene" in the way they were taught. Trust me, I don't want you to stand there weeping as you perform your audition song.

Please understand the distinction I am making. I'm talking about how something affects you and what you choose to do with it that makes a song active and engaging to watch and hear. As Paula Murray Cole says, so brilliantly, "Music is actually a rasa. It's the energy of the music that you let move into your body."

Take these emotions (pit stops) that you mapped out for yourself, and move *through* your feelings, so we can see you get to the other side of them. That is not emotional masturbation. Let the powerful flow of life move through you while you are singing.

Mixed Feelings

In another exercise in Paula's Rasaboxes class, where after I noticed the details of how I was feeling in one rasa (for example, *karuna,* which is sadness and compassion), I was asked to move into another (let's say *hasya,* which is laughter) to witness what it was like to move from one emotion to another. I let laughter move into my sadness very, very slowly. It started at 5 percent laughter/95 percent sadness, then 15 percent laughter, then 16 percent...then it was 28 percent laughter/72 percent sadness, then

40 percent laughter. If I didn't move from one feeling immediately, or quickly, into the other, I had the opportunity to feel my feelings as they changed! All sorts of unbelievable emotional details and textures came through on the way there. *Mixed feelings*...like bittersweetness. Laughter *and* sadness. Fear *and* disgust. Courage *and* wonder!

In the class Paula would question us to describe it: "How *much* courage and how *much* wonder? How does that percentage shift? Feelings are mixed, so you get to play with a palette of energy and emotion, a palette of sensations, with such *permissibility* to engage."

What do you see and feel on your way from one destination to the next? You don't just focus on the road, you also look around you. What colors are the leaves changing into? Does this town remind you of another? Are you still experiencing what your last destination was like? How does that affect the way you anticipate the next one? The act of moving through your feelings is now the action of the scene. Go for the ride! We will be right there with you, riding shotgun.

Moving through your feelings takes us on an emotional journey that is thrilling to watch!

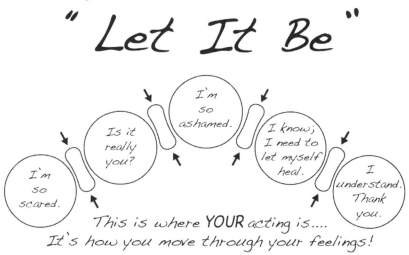

"*Let It Be*"

I'm so ashamed.

Is it really you?

I know; I need to let myself heal.

I'm so scared.

I understand. Thank you.

*This is where **YOUR** acting is....*
It's how you move through your feelings!

An astonishing example of a mixed feeling you might have as you travel from one destination to another in your song would be when you realize, "I'm still sad . . . but I think I'm going to be okay." Feelings are mixed, but *how* they mix with each other . . . now *that's* juicy! I encourage you to use and savor those moments on your journey.

Think of all the great actors you know who not only are successful, but to whom you are really *drawn*, actors who have made a difference onstage, on film, or on TV. Those actors aren't telling us how they feel. They are living in their feelings, moving through them with generosity, giving from the truest places within themselves. That is why we love them.

In the drawing, we take the roadmap and show the space in between destinations. To me, this is where your acting *really* takes place.

Welcome Michael Mayer, director of both *Spring Awakening* and *American Idiot.* We had a conversation in which he offered some great insights. I am so glad to include him in this chapter.

Michael: There's a propensity for actors to want to live in a primary color, because it feels good to them. But they deprive us of seeing all the texture and complexity they are capable of. Spice it up!

Sheri: Add a little more cumin and a pinch of curry!

Michael: Yes! I call this recipe acting. It's like you have one teaspoon of envy, and you really need a half a cup. If you don't give yourself the freedom to play in this way, it's a shame; it's so much fun to be able to do that.

Sheri: It is. It's playful!

Michael: But the really good feeling is the deep pleasure and deep joy of expressing yourself. It feels good to get this out. It's almost a sexual release! It's almost ecstatic! Where's the ecstasy? Where's the joy? Where's the love? There's buoyancy, a joy in the music making, even though the words can be dark and bitter. We are all the sons and daughters of rage and love. This is the yin and yang. You're pissed off, but you have so much love in you. Expressing a longing and a search, no matter how dark, has to come from love. You can't be open to receive the thing you're asking for if the request doesn't come from love. It's easy to hear the aggression in a song like *American Idiot,* and misinterpret it as an expression of pure rage. If the lyric says, "I don't want to be this," the implicit question is, what *do* you want to be? Feel the joy in the freedom of expressing your feelings.[7]

This comment, my friends, is a cordial invitation from Michael to experience your feelings fully, with detail and dynamics. While you are thinking about the "details of your feelings," don't you want people to know that you are a complex, cool, amazing person who has access to your feelings?

Not only is it cool to feel the ecstasy in expressing yourself, remember you are allowed to *love* to sing your song while you are singing it! And we will love you for that.

In Chapter 2, you learned a bit about the history of why people were the way they were in different decades and why they expressed themselves in the ways they did. You began to apply that understanding in how you styled the music in Chapter 6. As an actor, I now ask you to understand the history of why *you* are the way you are, and to apply this self-awareness to the story of your song with all the colors, flavors, and textures that make you uniquely you. Then please share it with us during your auditions.

Michael: If you have the history and you know why the song was written, how it was originally performed, why it connected to people when it first came out, and so on, then when you make a different choice, it's informed—and we know it. There's a decision being made. I learn volumes about what kind of performer that is. Immediately I'm interested. I want to keep listening. What I get is this person knows what they're talking about. They have a point of view. They're bringing their own intelligence, an idea, their own creativity, and a certain level of vulnerability. That's someone I want to work with, that's the kind of performer I want to work with for six weeks and make theater with. You have to bring your life experience into the room.

The Ride of Your Life

You must *always* take an emotional ride. And as you are rehearsing this song, try it ten different ways. Every time you do it, something new will happen: a new thought, a new texture, a new feeling, a different point of view, or a different story will arise. Why practice it so much? Because it's going to be a different ride every time depending on the show you're auditioning for and the roadmap you've drawn for yourself.

In the next chapter, I'm going to show you how to take this roadmap and apply it to all of the different genres of rock musicals that we discussed in the previous chapters.

8

How to Act a Rock Song

Do you know who Alfred Kinsey is? He was a biologist and professor of entomology and zoology who in 1947 founded the Kinsey Institute for Research in Sex, Gender, and Reproduction.[1] Kinsey did a tremendous amount of groundbreaking research on human sexuality, and created a *scandalous* scale that measures sexual orientation along a continuum. What he and his colleagues discovered by interviewing thousands of men and women about their sexuality is that few people have consistent behavior, thoughts, and feelings across time. Most of us have mixed levels of attraction to people of our own gender and the opposite gender.[2]

On the Kinsey Scale, being exclusively heterosexual, or "straight," was defined as 1. Being exclusively homosexual, or "gay," was defined as 6. Bisexuality—being equally attracted to men and women— was defined as 3. And there were other, varying degrees of sexual orientation between gay and straight along this continuum.

You get the point.

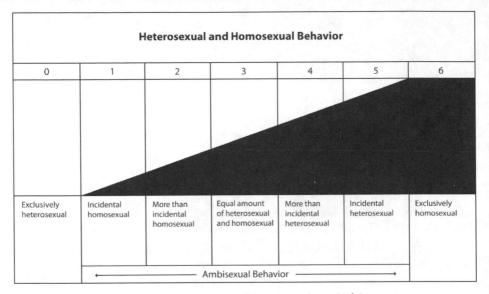

I have developed a theory, inspired by Kinsey's scale (shown above), on how to act a rock song. My adapted version of the Kinsey Scale, which goes from 1–5, looks like a dial.

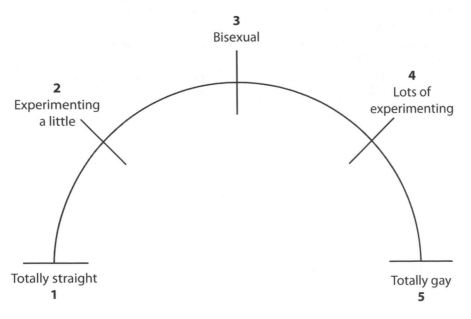

The thing to remember when you are looking at my dial is that it's not exact. It's not about numbers. It's about measuring sexuality as it relates to your performance.

"How on God's green earth will this help me act?" you may ask.

I would like to preface the material in this chapter by saying that I am a gay woman. A lesbian. And I am active in the gay and lesbian community. When I refer to being "totally gay," or to being gay in any way at all, understand that the term is held in the deepest reverence humanly possible. Being "totally gay" with regard to acting a rock song means the story is fully realized with the deepest level of creativity possible. I love being gay, and I hope that you love, accept, and respect everyone regardless of their sexual orientation. Please don't use any part of my adaptation of the Kinsey Scale to hurt or judge anyone. We are *all* special creatures.

The Sheri Sanders Theory of Sexuality in Pop/Rock Musicals

Here is my theory. You're going to flip out.

Remember when we said that rock songs aren't attached to an already existing story? Well, since they aren't, they stand on their own, which also means there's nothing that defines how a song is "supposed" to be handled. As an actor, you now have to intuit how to *perform* a song, *and* you have to know how to make your song *fit* the genre and the era like a glove.

There are many different ways to act a rock song. You can do a song totally straight by leaving the lyrics alone and letting your emotions tell the story. Seeing that the lyrics are so strong that you can take them literally to the point of it being comedic makes it "totally gay." Similar to the Kinsey Scale, there are varying degrees in between.

Doing a Song "Totally Straight" (1 on the Dial)

"Don't act it, just stand there and sing it." Have you ever received this feedback from a casting director or a teacher when you sang a rock song? Of course, people don't really mean it literally when they say it. Standing and singing without doing *anything* would be a lousy performance to watch. What they really mean is, "Don't act as if you are singing a show tune."

It's true. Performers often try to act a rock song just like they'd act a legit musical theater song—and that's really bad! Rock music is *not* the same as legit. If you're like most actors, you have been trained to *show us* how you feel—rather than letting us, the audience, perceive it for ourselves—and so you are doing waaaay too much for rock.

Having been told to "stand there and sing it," you might respond, "Okay, but what do I do with myself instead?"

This is a really good question. How does one act by "doing nothing"?

When I asked casting director Cindi Rush this question, her reply was, "You're in a musical, so you are playing a character. You have to find that way of evoking the feeling that we have when we listen to someone on the radio, and also be a character without sacrificing the truth of the acting part."[3]

Well said!

There are certain songs, and certain *kinds* of songs, that must be done straight. Such songs are simple in sentiment, simple in arrangement, and deliver simple messages. When you realize you have one of these songs on your hands, from now on, put no story on it. Add no scenario. Just allow yourself to feel the essence of the song and then move through your feelings while you are singing. For something so simple, it is incredibly powerful to watch. You can trust that your feelings, if they are honest, will be riveting.

Don't make the story more than it is. Leave the song alone, and let it tell the story for you. If you let the lyrics do the talking, it will speak for itself. Your job is to get out of the way of the energy of the song and be present in it. Go along for an emotional ride. The audience needn't know how you feel. Only *you* need to know how you feel.

Songs to Do "Totally Straight"

What songs would be great to do totally straight? How about these:

- ▶ "Imagine" written and sung by John Lennon
- ▶ "Dust in the Wind" by Kansas (written by Kerry Livgren)
- ▶ "Pride in the Name of Love" by U2 (about Martin Luther King Jr.)
- ▶ "Angels" by Robbie Williams (co-written by Williams and Guy Chambers)
- ▶ "Broken Wing" by Martina McBride (co-written by Phil Barnhart, Sam Hogan, and James House)
- ▶ "LA Song" written and sung by Beth Hart

If you notice, songs like these are sung out to the universe, not to a specific person. But in feeling your feelings, don't get wishy-washy with your focus. You *need whoever is out there* to hear you.

The Art of Evoking Emotion

The next question I have for you has been earth-shattering for many of my students. If listening to Paul McCartney singing "Let It Be" evokes emotions in you, what if your singing could do the same for someone else? What if your connection to your emotions gave you the power to evoke emotions in other people?

How does one evoke emotions in other people?

If you are clear about how *you* feel, then that gives your listeners permission to feel what *they* feel about their own lives. What you are actually doing is acknowledging the purpose of music, which is sharing who you are without judgment. Singing the song will become an experience that is both uniquely yours and universal at the same time. If you connect to your feelings the way the artists that we love on the radio do, then your audience gets to be affected by you, just like you have been affected.

Your goal is to evoke emotions in your listeners, which, in the case of a rock musical audition is the creative team. As Paula Murray Cole, says, "Be in who you are and how you feel. By doing this you are allowing the witnesses to taste the juiciness because you are so filled with it."[4]

Michael McElroy shared something with me that I want you to keep in your mind as you walk in the room for your audition. He said:

> Remember the days when you got a new album? You'd invite a group of friends over and you'd go up to your room, put the record on and listen to it? You'd share the musical experience by feeling the songs together. There used to be a community, and a sense of connectedness. We listened and loved music together. We no longer have that. We've lost something important in the way in which we experience music. We have iPods and iTunes now. We put on our headphones and listen to music while we walk down the street or download it by ourselves at home. Listening to music is now an isolating experience.[5]

Can you imagine coming into the audition room and sharing your rock song in a way that would cause the people in the room to feel a sense of community again? Could you sing it in a way that they feel you are not separate from them, and instead feel that you are all sharing the song together? Hanging out together? Being with each other and loving the song together?

What we were back in the day is who we need to be again when we audition. We need to share. Now this advice doesn't just go for singing a song totally straight. That goes for everything that follows on the dial: every genre of rock musical, every musical, every relationship, every everything. But here's a great place to start.

When you share your love for the song in this way, the creative team will say, "Oh my god, I love that song! I haven't heard it since

I was thirteen in the back seat of my mom's station wagon. I was thirteen and in *love* with Kenny Winkleman. I can still smell the vinyl. Wow! What a beautiful and intelligent performer." Or "Oh my god, *that song!* Where is that song from? I know that feeling . . . call them back."

Always be mindful that you are giving them a gift, *the gift of their own juiciness, their* feelings, *their* memories. Casting directors are so busy that they rarely get to have a moment like this in life, let alone in the audition room. And they'll feel grateful for it, grateful to you for coming in and caring enough about them to let them have an experience of themselves.

Most of the time, we only think of the people behind the table as the people who can make us famous and save us from destroying ourselves by hiring us. So we shove ourselves down their throats. How do I know? I've done it, darling. And it doesn't work. You need to treat this moment as if you were "sharing the specificity of universality."

We are all the same at the end of the day. Who can *you* be that allows others to be who *they* are? When you are being this onstage, hearts open to you and the audience is immediately engaged. So stand there, sing the song, feel your feelings, and share them as a gift for anyone within earshot.

Why is this so important?

It is an act of generosity.

Alaine Alldaffer, the casting director at Playwrights Horizons, is one of the coolest kids in town. She's got "old-school" class, and it is evident that she cares about the wellness of actors inside the audition room and out. "If you come in with the spirit of generosity, gratitude, and contribution, you can't be nervous. There's no room for that. When it's not about you, there's no room for fear. Generosity is not based in fear. Are you going to live in fear? Or in how blessed you are? Give your joy, give your pain. Just give. That's when I say, 'Oh my God, I love my job!' People make my day when I feel their generosity. I say thank you and it's sincere."[6]

That, my friend, is how you do it totally straight. And knowing this, how would you do "Let It Be" right now? Go back to the emotional roadmap of the song as defined in Chapter 7, and perform it totally straight.

Don't skip over trying this out. Really do it, as it is a super fun exercise and will prove to you how powerful doing a song totally straight can be with the right song.

Doing a Song "Totally Gay" (5 on the Dial)

Way over on the other end of the spectrum, a rock song that begs to be done humorously is one that we call "totally gay."

I am using the phrase "totally gay" as the highest compliment possible. Used as a teaching device to show actors how to demonstrate an exciting and profound flair for the dramatic, this distinction has proven to work like a charm. Again, please use this tool respectfully.

The gay end of the spectrum of human sexuality as it exists in pop/rock musicals represents fully realized storytelling in fully realized scenarios. If you choose to do a song totally gay, you will be taking a clear, strong storyline that is already present in the song and dramatizing it. The lyrics of the rock song will give you all the hints you need to establish a clever and creative point of view.

So how exactly can you take a dramatic story and fully realize it so that it comes across as a big, beautiful, colorful, comedic scene? You do it by taking yourself and your circumstances *literally*— meaning at face value.

Over the years I have put comedic spins of rock songs "on" my students that have proven successful time and time again at making people behind the table laugh. What if "It's All Coming Back to Me Now" by Celine Dion could be performed as a woman who has amnesia and is desperately trying to recall spending the night with a man who is insisting they've slept together?

What if you were singing "It's Raining Men" by the Weather Girls and it was *really* raining men? Are they falling out of the sky? What would you do if they were? How would you react in that situation? How would you feel about this occurrence? And how would you dramatize it? Those are the kinds of questions you must ask yourself when doing a song totally gay.

What if you sang Britney Spears's song "Toxic," and pretended you were Britney Spears performing at the American Music Awards ceremony and you noticed you were getting sick during your performance, and then even sicker as the song goes on? What if you then realized that a man you were "addicted to" was emotionally toxic and he was the reason you were getting sick? The lyrics of the song could support this interpretation, and it would be funny if you treated the idea literally.

How about the song "Superstition" by Stevie Wonder? What if you were not only superstitious, but worse . . . paranoid? What if you think terrible things are going to happen to you, and then they do? A ladder is going to fall on you. You go to hold a baby and find out that it is thirteen months old! Then you've broken a mirror and you'll get seven years of bad luck. How does this affect you? Your paranoia grows as you sing the song because one thing after another keeps happening.

How about "Tempted" by the group Squeeze? The chorus is "tempted by the fruit of another." What if you were to ask the piano player to place a banana (that you've brought into the audition room) on the piano when you are ready to start, and then you act like that banana belongs to the piano player? It looks delicious, and you are tempted to eat it. You have to struggle with this feeling throughout the song. Signal to him, as if you are asking, "Is this your banana?" That could be really, really funny for an audition.

Before you begin, remember, you *must* ask the piano player if he is comfortable placing a banana on the piano for you at the beginning of the song. If he says no, then you do it. If you are auditioning for a *high comedy* musical, though, the pianist should know the kind of performers who are coming in and expect them to do outrageous things like this, so they *are* likely to agree.

At no point should you ever ask the accompanist to engage with you as a performer *inside* the actual song. If you ask the pianist if that's his banana, assume that his lack of response to you means *it isn't his banana* and therefore it's free for you to eat (even though it's not yours). Peel that banana, savor it, and take a bite right on the button of the song.

You must look at the stories that songs are telling and wonder, "What kind of story is in here? Can I make it funny? What does it need to be to get a laugh? How far do I need to take it in order for it to work? How literally should I play it?"

A successful comedy audition depends on your point of view, or what I call your point of *YOU*.

Larry O'Keefe, the composer and lyricist of a numbers of musicals, including *Bat Boy, Legally Blonde,* and *Heathers,* is a really funny writer. I spoke with him to see if he had any advice on auditioning. He said,

> My goal is to make people laugh. Because I'm lazy, I found the easiest way to do that is build a story which takes convincing characters and plunges them into ridiculous or extreme situations. The songs show up at moments of greatest peril, highest stakes, biggest cliffhangers, whether literal or emotional. That makes it easy to write songs where people sing passionately. There's many ways to write entertaining musicals—farces, epics, and jukebox shows with or without plot—but the only method I really know is to put the story first and the music and lyrics in service of that.
>
> Kerry Butler came in and auditioned for *Bat Boy*. She sang "I Will Survive," which was made famous by Gloria Gaynor, and we went, "Uh oh: what could a beautiful suburban-looking white girl have to say with this song?" But she killed it. She didn't try to sound like Gloria

Gaynor, she came off almost like Jennifer Aniston from *Friends,* a heartbroken, vengeful, wounded, proud, rocking Jennifer Aniston. She was completely committing, straight-faced, to the emotion of the song, but made it hilarious by applying the lyrics to a (realistic) character you'd never think of as singing this song. It came off as loopy in the first verse, but by the end it was triumphant too.[7]

Of course, I had to call Kerry Butler and ask her what she did to prepare her audition song. Kerry, who is an accomplished comedic actress, said:

I did the song kind of against how it's usually done. I broke it down like a monologue. I made up a real story that was going on. I pretended the person was sitting there and he had to hear me.

I really made it my own. So I did it very talky at the start. "At first I was afraid," like I really was afraid. No, really, "I was petrified!" and I told him how I felt about everything he did. And I built it energetically.

When it got to the lyrics "Go on now, go," I pretended he was trying to explain himself to me and I put my fingers in my ears, and I was like "Lalalalala, I can't hear you!" I created an imaginary interaction between me and the person with whom I was having this experience. It was how I let the person affect me that made it interesting. I was doing everything I could not to cry. So much, in fact, that it was funny.

Then I chose to gain back my dignity. I started dancing and marching around the room celebrating my power. It was a very serious situation for me.[8]

Kerry has a recommendation for you, and I hope you will heed her words. She booked *Bat Boy* from that audition and because of her "rock sense humor," has played some of our favorite characters on Broadway: Kira in *Xanadu,* Penny in *Hairspray,* Sherrie in *Rock of Ages,* and Audrey in *Little Shop of Horrors.* She says, "Sometimes you're going to fail. But you can't be afraid to make a mistake. You can't be afraid to bomb. It's like a gage. Go all the way with it, so that you can see what works and what doesn't work. It will work more often than it will fail. But only if you do it 100 percent. You have to."

She concludes, "Some songs aren't right. You just can't make them funny. You have to look for songs that already have a strong a point of view. A lot of songs can be made funny. When you're auditioning and you do something different than it's normally done, they'll think 'This is a thinking actor.' They'll think you'll bring something creative to the table when they hire you because you are doing something that no one else does: you are using your imagination."9

Back to Larry O'Keefe! He says,

I think reversed realities also make it easy to be funny. It's the dissonance, the paradox. But it should be realistic to the character you choose. A normal person in a ridiculous situation or an extraordinary person stranded in an ordinary world: that can make for great comedy and you can build those stories in a single song.

The Wedding Singer (music by Matthew Sklar, book and lyrics by Chad Beguelin and Tim Herlihy) is an underappreciated show. It's both a love story and a 1980s homage. The writers of that show deliberately chose to emulate different styles of pop. There's a "Cyndi Lauper" song, a "New Edition" song, a "Culture Club" song. But they're not commenting on it just to do it; the characters are all placed in situations that are very real to them. The songs are not parodies. The characters don't know they're doing a homage, they're trying to get love or make money or get over heartbreak. The humor is in sincerity.

The movie Heathers was an antidote to the myths promoted by the John Hughes movies of the '80s, myths like "the nerd can win the cheerleader" and "teenagers will all drop their hostility and get along if given a chance." Heathers instead told a hard truth: seventeen-year-olds have no incentive to stop being cruel to each other. They're all crammed in a lifeboat in freezing waters, and if you don't want to be pushed out you'd better push someone else.

For my new musical version of Heathers we're keeping the heightened colors and styles of the era but we're not deliberately doing a pastiche of any particular '80s song or sound. Yes, our cliques will wear shoulder pads and big hair, but deep down they are terrified, troubled girls hanging on by their fingernails, capable of violence because that's what fear and competition can drive you to. The humor comes from the extremity and the irony, not from falsity or insincerity or pop culture references.

When I audition actors for these characters, I'll be looking for deep sincerity and high energy. My hope is you'll show me the most basic emotions of cruelty, hope, hatred, and love. The deepest, scariest, most wonderful emotions. The story must be true to you. Don't comment on the song or the character or high school or the late '80s; you should be the person, and then amplify the emotions till they make me go "whoa." Be grounded in sincerity blown up to epic proportions.

I also love characters that are cheerfully oblivious to their own nature. No matter what the medium, I love cheerfulness. I love a happy idiot with a great plan. Will Ferrell plays wonderful happy idiots. He means well. A lot of rock music doesn't contain happy idiots. The emotions that embody rock are "let go and have a great time," not "I have an amazing plan." But they can coexist in the same show or the same character. There's no reason to give up on one or the other. Kerry Butler managed to accomplish both in a single song.

Oh . . . and please don't take an existing song and rewrite the lyrics. I'll only notice the writing, and I will completely miss your performing skills.[10]

Songs to Do Totally Gay

What songs would you do totally gay? Go look 'em up, and try 'em out!
▶ "Don't Play That Song for Me" by Aretha Franklin (written by Ahmet Ertegun and Betty Nelson)
▶ "I Feel the Earth Move" written and performed by Carole King
▶ "Man Eater" written and performed by Daryl Hall and John Oates (about actress Kelly LeBrock)
▶ "How Will I Know?" by Whitney Houston (co-written by George Merrill and Shannon Rubicam from Boy Meets Girl)

How to Be Totally Gay Emotionally

Let's use "So Emotional" by Whitney Houston as an example of how to create a totally gay performance. I will walk you through the same process as the last chapter, but this time combining emotional mapping with the Kinsey Scale. Begin by taking a look at the lyrics and identifying an emotion you would feel if the line was literally true rather than metaphoric.

I've been hearing your heartbeat inside of me
I keep your photograph beside my bed
Living in a world of fantasies
I can't get you out of my head

If I look at the first set of *these* lyrics, what I notice in the story is that I am *obsessing* about this guy.
(Anxious excitement)

I remember the way that we touch
I think: You feel soooo good.
(Desire)

I wish I didn't like it so much

But you're soooo bad for me.
(Crazy-making)

I get so emotional, baby

I feel really emotional and hyper- sensitive!
(Weepy)

Every time I think of you
I get so emotional, baby

It makes me feel crazy!
(Excited)

Ain't it shocking what love can do

I had no idea I had this in me.
(Shocked)

Ain't it shocking what love can do? Ain't it shocking what love can do

Wow, I feel better getting my feelings out.
(Amazed and delighted)

Take a look at the emotional map that follows. I'm giving you an emotional map with a clue on the tone you could take in your performance. But then it will be up to you. How emotional are you? What emotions are you having? Does the man you are singing to make you weep uncontrollably, or does he make you do crazy things that you had no idea you had in you? What are those things? What kind of obsessive behaviors? The lyrics say that it's *shocking* what love can do. Shocking in what way? Is your love surprising? Did you not know you had it in you?

See if the map I've laid out would work for you.

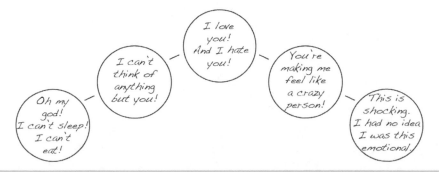

How are you digging all of this? Crazy, right? In practice, it works like a charm.

Doing a Song Bisexually (3 on the Dial)

Before we move on, it's important to clarify the difference between doing something totally gay and doing something bisexual. As you are about to see, both approaches can be funny.

When doing songs totally gay (5 on the Kinsey Scale), you are a storyteller first and foremost, engaging the lyrics fully in an imagined scenario. With bisexual songs, you are split right down the middle between capturing the essence of the era you are portraying and being a storyteller. There's a simple analogy for it. Say you were having a love affair with someone. The feelings are very real regardless of what era they are in, but a love affair that happens in a disco club is undeniably different than one that happens at a civil rights march, or at a high school dance in the '50s, or at a Def Leppard concert.

At 3 on the Kinsey Scale, there is a perfect balance between capturing the essence of the time period *and* telling a personal story.

Songs to Do Bisexually

I love to use the '80s era, the disco era, the era of the '50s and '60s, and emo music as great examples of bisexuality. See how the possibilities are endless. Tunes that can be played as "bi" include:

► "Jimmy Mack" by Martha and the Vandellas (written by Holland-Dozier-Holland)

► "Don't Leave Me This Way" by Thelma Houston (written by Kenneth Gamble, Leon Huff, and Cary Gilbert)

► "Look Away" by Chicago (written by Diane Warren)

► "Email My Heart" by Britney Spears (written by Eric Foster White)

Whether you are a boy or a girl, for a rock musical like *Rock of Ages* pretend you are a 1980s rock star and this audition represents your 1980s rock video. You have on imaginary skin-tight acid-washed jeans, big hair, and a full face of makeup. You take your rock stardom very seriously. You think you're really hot—the hottest, actually. So throw the audience sexy looks—dirty, even. Play the air guitar. Do crazy things with your tongue. Purse your lips. Blow neon kisses into the imaginary camera lens. That's how to capture the essence of the '80s.

The cool thing about singing a song from the '80s in your auditions for rock musicals like *Rock of Ages* or even *Xanadu* is that you are making fun of that era while also honoring it. That is what those shows are about.

For now, know this: some of the most popular singers from the '80s were super silly by nature. They were emotionally *and* vocally melodramatic! Of course, back then, singing this way was the thing to do. Now it is your job to honor the way they were and what they chose to do! Take the songs they sang and embellish them by taking their melodrama and the silly things they did with their voices and doing it twice as melodramatic and silly as they did!

But be very serious about how you sing your song. Be fully committed to it! Don't comment on it. You can't think you're silly. Watch videos of well-known '80s artists, and study the way they express their feelings. Taylor Dayne's "Tell It to My Heart," "I Still Believe" by Brenda K. Starr, and "Workin' for the Weekend" by Loverboy "Sunglasses at Night" Corey Hart are prime examples. Study their mannerisms and their vocals, and incorporate these into your performance.

I asked my friend Michael Minarik, a lead producer and cast member of *Rock of Ages,* what chemistry he thinks would be necessary to produce a winning audition for the show. According to him, it takes two things to have a good audition for *Rock of Ages:* thinking outside the box and honesty. "Comedy is honesty in absurd situations," he says. "When I am playing Lonny and sing 'I Can't Fight this Feeling Anymore' to Dennis, I am not commenting on how absurd this situation is—I am being honest with him that this feeling of a 'bromance' has been inside me and I have to tell him through this song. Honesty is the key. People who 'play the funny' don't really get the medium *Rock of Ages* lives in. It's a fine line, but straddling it makes it all the more enjoyable." As an afterthought, he adds, "Oh, and ripped jeans and a killer mullet might help as well."[11]

Here's an example of how you might do an audition for a show in this era, using "Here I Go Again" (although this song is actually in *Rock of Ages,* which means you cannot use it to audition for *Rock of Ages,* it is good as a teaching example).

Let's say you're at a bar (leaning on the piano) and feeling bad about yourself. You start to hear a song on the jukebox and you think, "Hey, I know this song. You start to enjoy it and to express how it feels in your body. The next thing you know, you are now the lead singer of Whitesnake, rocking it out onstage at a bar in Secaucus, New Jersey, feeling extraordinarily good and no longer in a shitty mood. That's how you could perform the song bisexually.

Another perfect era of bisexuality is the disco era. If you are auditioning for *Priscilla, Queen of the Desert* or *Sister Act,* I want you to feel what it would be like if you were a disco queen (male or female, of course) onstage in a discotheque in the late '70s or early '80s, and you had been brought there specifically to lift people out of their seats and get them out on the dance floor where they could forget their cares by getting down and boogying. The disco ball is spinning, you are feeling the music in your body, *and* you are having feelings about what you are singing about. So if you sang "Don't Leave Me this Way" by Thelma Houston in this setting, you would feel your feelings ("Don't leave me, I love you"), and as the music started to build, you would say, "You can't leave me. Look how beautiful I am. I can get a room full of people off their butts and onto the dance floor. I am amazing!"

I spoke with Alex Timbers, playwright and director of *Bloody Bloody Andrew Jackson,* about why his brilliant show falls into the category of bisexuality. He said,

> Emo music traffics in overwrought passions and in displaying how deep and kaleidoscopic the singer's emotions are. But the emotionality is so overwrought that it can easily become comedic, which is the realm that *Bloody Bloody Andrew Jackson* loves to explore. It's not like *American Idiot,* which is appropriately sincere in its youthful anger. *Bloody Bloody Andrew Jackson* lives in two places: it is both genuine in its angst but simultaneously so over-the-top that it can allow itself to be humorous. That self-awareness is key, and it's what makes emo the perfect music genre for today's zeitgeist, where we love work that is both ironic and sincere, like *The Daily Show*. The music is so sincere that it's silly, yet it's so simple in its emotions that it can be profoundly moving. The style is not cheeky or campy like *Rock of Ages* or *Urinetown*. It's about a deadpan Will Ferrell-like commitment to absurd circumstances and being able to balance the comedy with genuine depth of anger and hurt and desire. We are looking for an actor who may not "kill it" vocally, but who is a fantastic storyteller, and who can play the humor so close to the vest that they never tip it into musical comedy land.[12]

The bisexuality of the show emerges from how it is covering two different worlds, the comic and the tragic, at the same time. We couldn't call it totally gay because there is no scenario being played out with your lyrics. You are merely expressing yourself emotionally.

When you are auditioning for a '50s musical, examples of the kind of image I want to see from your portrayal is as follows: If you are a guy, I want you to imagine you are a teen heartthrob. You have come out onstage at *The Ed Sullivan Show* to croon to an audience full of screaming teenagers. Find one special girl in the audience, single her out, and sing your love to her. How does she react? Does she faint? How does it make you feel? How do all the other girls react to that? By doing your song in this manner, you are creating a perfect 1950s picture, capturing the essence of the period, and creating an actual scene.

Now, you don't have to play this exact scenario. It is one out of many kinds of scenarios that took place during this era. You could also pretend that you're at a record shop. You could be at a drive-in. You could be a dancer on *American Bandstand*. What I want is for you to give me a sense of the era and have your feelings.

If you are a woman, the scenario is similar. Walk out to the center of the stage, carrying yourself with poise, and feel the spotlight on you, like you are onstage at *The Ed Sullivan Show*. Then feel two backup singers standing behind you, literally "backing you up" emotionally while you sing about how your boyfriend left you alone at the dance and you're too good for that kind of treatment. Is it your first time on *Ed Sullivan*? Are you nervous? Excited? And this boy you're singing about . . . what are the details you know about him? Did he "pin" you with his class pin? Were you going steady? Was he your first love? What did he do to you? What are the details? Take us into the time period, and have your feelings too. Never sacrifice one for the other.

Let's use our '50s and '60s tune, "Please Mr. Postman" by the Marvelettes.

Take a look at my story. Based upon how I have configured the emotional roadmap, what feelings do you feel when you listen to the song? Again, this is my interpretation.

Stop! Oh yes, wait a minute Mr. Postman
Wait! Mr. Postman

I see "Stop!" and "Wait!" And that reads like I am very anxious to speak with him!
(Anxious)

So many days you've passed me by
You saw the tears standing in my eyes

I think: You never notice me, even when I cry.
(Abandoned)

You wouldn't stop to make me feel better
By leaving me a card or a letter

You know (because you never stop by here) that I'm waiting to hear from my boyfriend
(Lonely)

Please Mister Postman, look and see
Is there a letter, oh yeah, in your bag for me
You know it's been so long
Yeah, since I heard from this boyfriend of mine

I desire so much to hear from him.
 (Desire)

You'd better
Wait a minute/Wait a minute

Please! Don't go.
(Needy)

Oh, you'd better
Wait a minute/Wait a minute
Please Mister Postman,
Deliver the letter/The sooner the better.

I desperately need you!
(Desperation)

Kissing Girls/Kissing Boys (2 on the Dial): Experimenting with the Same Sex

Now for the place on the Kinsey Scale that I call "experimenting." Into this category would fall a woman who says, "I love kissing women. I don't think I can have a relationship with one, but they're fun and sweet to kiss!" or a man who says the same thing about other men.

   Story-wise, your song would fit into this space on the dial between totally straight and bisexuality if you were going to stand here and sing it, letting the emotional life and a message flow through you simply, while you direct the song to a specific person.

This requires you actually to see a human being and share the feelings you are having with him or her. If you just stood there and felt the essence of the song, but sang it to the universe, it would seem foolish in this scenario. It is a slightly more dramatic mode of storytelling, to incorporate a scene partner (imaginary) into the performance.

In terms of how much to act the song, I would say to err on the side of "feeling your feelings" than to do too much. Don't act it. Just give your feelings to this imaginary scene partner.

Songs for Experimental Sexuality

Tunes that would be a perfect 2 on the dial include:

► "You're No Good" covered by Linda Ronstadt (written by Clint Ballard Jr.)
► "Cry Baby" covered in 1970 by Janis Joplin (co-written by Jerry Ragovoy and Burt Burns)
► "Goodbye to You" by Scandal (written by Zack Smith)
► "A Song for You" by Donny Hathaway (written by Leon Russell)

Experimenting a Little

Here's how to do "In Love with a Girl" by Gavin DeGraw where it is at the "experimenting" part of the scale.

I wanna tell you what you do to thank you practiced what you preach,
And now I know there's nothing we can't reach,
'cause the heart can't erase once it finds a place to be warm and welcome,
To be held and sheltered

It begins with me being thankful for this woman because she taught me about myself.
(Gratitude)

I'm in love with a girl who knows me better,
Fell for the woman just when I met her,

I've been passionately in love with her since I met her.
(Passionate)

Took my sweet time when I was bitter,

I was a total jerk to her.
(Shame)

Someone understands,

And she loved me anyway.

(I feel cherished)

And she knows how to treat a fella right,
Gives me that feeling every night,
Wants to make love when I wanna fight,

The sex is awesome, too!

(Satisfaction)

Now someone understands me!

She really gets me.

(Gratitude)

Do this exactly the same way as you did "Let It Be," except directed to someone, which makes it a 2 on the dial.

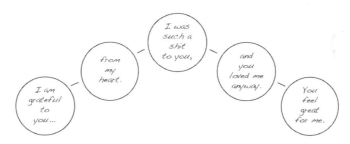

"In Love with a Girl"

I am grateful to you... *from my heart.* *I was such a shit to you,* *and you loved me anyway.* *You feel great for me.*

How do *you* take this ride?

Brigadoon (4 on the Dial)

This kind of experimenting is very close to where I am in real life. Except that instead of considering myself straight and I experiment with other girls, I consider myself gay. Then on occasions—when I am between serious relationships with girlfriends—I have been known to have fun with a guy. Of course, this is kind of like the story of *Brigadoon* (the musical). The day I experiment with a man is a magical day that happens on the order of once every hundred years. Then he's gone, vanishing into the mist like the town of Brigadoon, without a trace of ever having been there.

If you are going to audition for a rock musical that is dramatic, such as *Chess* or *Jesus Christ Superstar,* this is where your song needs to lie. The space in between bisexuality and being totally gay, which I lovingly refer to as Brigadoon (4 on the Kinsey Scale), represents high drama, focusing on lyrics, no comedy necessary!

Songs for Brigadoon

The following songs are naturally dramatic because the music is sweeping and emotional, with a strong story.

▶ "Don't Stop Me Now" by Queen
▶ "Come Sail Away" by Styx
▶ "Bat Out of Hell" by Meatloaf
▶ "To Love You More" by Celine Dion

Spending Time in Brigadoon

Let use "What's Up?" by Linda Perry as an example of a rock song done Brigadoon-style. Here are the lyrics with an emotional roadmap added to them.

Twenty-five years and my life is still
Trying to get up that great big hill of hope
For a destination

I see "Trying to get up that great big hill of hope" and I think I'm struggling to succeed.
(Failure)

I realized quickly as I knew I should
That this world was made up of this brotherhood of man
For whatever that means

I feel like no one has ever been there for me.
(Loneliness)

And so I cry sometimes
When I'm lying in bed
Just to get it all out
What's in my head
And I, I am feeling a little peculiar

I feel overwhelmed by my emotions and I don't know how to get a hold of them.
(Feeling out of control)

And so I wake in the morning
And I step outside

And I take a deep breath and I get real high
And I scream at the top of my lungs
What's going on?

I need to get high so I can get out of this bad head space.
(Wild)

And I say, hey hey
I said hey, what's going on?

I ask the universe for help, and no one responds.
(Abandoned)

And I say, hey hey
I said hey, what's going on?

And so I ask again.
(Desperate to be heard)

Twenty-five years and my life is still
Trying to get up that great big hill of hope
For a destination

I decide, "I'll make it through this."
(Resigned, but hopeful)

Now, take a look at the roadmap.

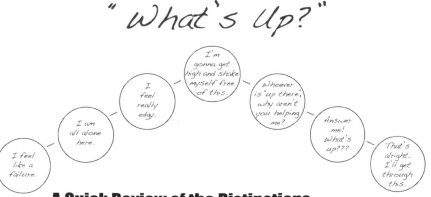

A Quick Review of the Distinctions on the Kinsey Scale of Acting

Going from totally straight (1) to totally gay (5), here are the basics for identifying where your song needs to lie on the scale as an actor.

1. *Totally straight:* Stand there and sing; just feel the essence
2. *Kissing girls/kissing boys of the same gender as you:* Sing to someone in particular; feel the essence

3. *Bisexual:* Half essence of the time period, half storytelling
4. *Brigadoon:* High drama, no comedy
5. *Totally gay:* High drama, high comedy

Make sense? Here's a visual in case you need to see it.

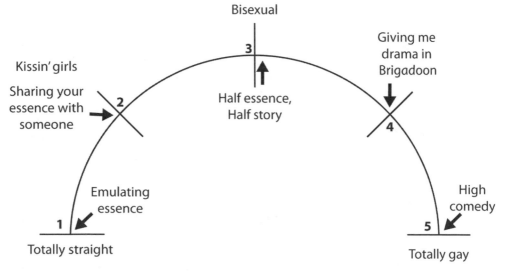

Now that you understand my dial and all the different ways to act a rock song, know that developing your intuition about which one is appropriate is the most important part of this whole experience. It is *your responsibility* to understand where your song lies on the continuum. Some songs, like some people, are at varying degrees of sexuality. So are some musicals.

Do you want to know why I created this scale? Several years ago, I had a disastrous audition for *Mary Poppins* on Broadway. I did a comedic interpretation of "Gimme Gimme" from *Thoroughly Modern Millie* in which I did the song as if I was on a shopping spree that was intended for retail therapy. My version of the song was totally gay, a 5, when I really needed to be kissing girls, a 2. As you can probably imagine, it did *not* go over well with the creative team.

You must know where your rock song needs to be on the dial so that you won't get a response of "Gross . . . she's acting too much" or "Well, he missed a really great opportunity to be playful." That's why working with the dial always leads actors to greater success.

As important as it is to know where your song rests on the dial, you also need to know that even though it lies in a particular place on the scale, it doesn't have to live there forever. You can bend your song from one number, one form of "sexuality," to another depending on the show for which you are auditioning. For example, if you were going to sing "In Love with a Girl" in an audition for *American Idiot,* you would sing it totally straight. The tone of *American Idiot* is that all emotions are out on the table, so singing out to the universe is appropriate. That's a 1 on the dial.

You could also sing "In Love with a Girl" directly to the girl about whom you are talking. Then it would work for a show like *Next to Normal.* The approach would be a 2 on the dial; kissing girls or, in this case, kissing boys!

If you take that same song and hold all your feelings inside, trying to keep them from us and being tortured internally by them, that same song becomes right for *Bloody Bloody Andrew Jackson.* Then the song is bisexual, a 3 on my dial.

Here's a second song example, "So Emotional." To me, "So Emotional" naturally is high comedy, just as we worked on it. Thus it's a 5 on the dial, making it appropriate for *Shrek* and *Heathers.*

But what if you were auditioning for *Mamma Mia* with it? Where would you put it on the Kinsey Scale then? And how would you act it? Personally, I would put it at kissing girls, 2 on the dial. You would be positive, up, light, and feeling the good emotions you would have if you were getting married on a Greek island. If it were for *The Wedding Singer*, you would be bisexual with it, putting it at a 3 on the scale. Let me show you what this would look like on the dial. The little balls I placed on the dial are where there are other possible ways of performing a song.

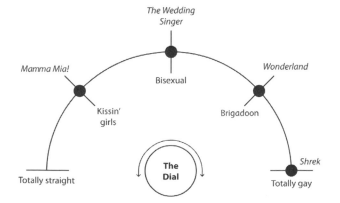

"Let It Be" is totally straight and should be done as a 1 on the dial if you audition with it for *Hair*. But even this sweet, simple song can be transformed into a totally gay version. Here's how. Rest a cupcake on the edge of the piano. Put it on a small plate. Walk away from it. Struggle with your desire to eat it: first you're going to eat it, and then you're going to abstain. Finally, you sing the last "let it be," and then you'd say in your speaking voice, "in my mouth," and eat it.

Get it? Let it be *in my mouth.*

That would be a 5 on the dial. But please note: most casting directors hate props. So you can only do this if you are auditioning for a *high comedy*.

Now, let's look at "What's Up?" It tells a pretty dramatic story. It's real. And you have to be a fully engaged storyteller for us to understand the depth of the struggle you are having in this world. Brigadoon, baby!

But let me ask you: In the song, there's a line that says, "And so I wake in the morning and I step outside and I take a deep breath and I get real high and I scream from the top of my lungs what's going on?" Imagine that in that moment you actually got high. You don't have to fake smoking a doobie or anything; your energy just has to change in the way that you imagine getting stoned would make you change. In making this adjustment, the experience changes; it becomes heightened and funny. Playing the song places it on the end of the Kinsey Scale, at 5, which is as gay as it can get.

Funny is honest. It's sincere. Please always ensure that you come from your truth. You can also be very funny *and* very touching all in the same song.

What else could you do with "What's Up?" You could turn the song into a 1980s rocker chick tune, tease up your hair, and use it in an audition for *Rock of Ages*. That's bi.

You could sing it to someone for *Next to Normal, Rent,* or *Spiderman.* And we're back to kissing girls at a level 2 on the Kinsey Scale.

"Please Mr. Postman" is perfect where it is, in the land of bisexuality, for shows like *Hairspray, All Shook Up,* and *Cry Baby.* But if you want to bring it over to kissing girls, at 2, it would also be a great audition song for *The Marvelous Wonderettes, Shout, Bee Hive, Leader of the Pack,* or *Smokey Joe's Café.*

Totally straight, it's ideal for *Jersey Boys,* where the team wants to hear you sing a song in the style of the '50s, with no acting, just emulating the essence of the era. That's at a 1 on the dial.

An "Alternative" Interpretation

Just so you guys can see that there are so many ways a song can be interpreted, I wanted to show you a totally different interpretation of a song we already did, "Please Mr. Postman." This is the interpretation you will see when you watch the final performance on the DVD. It has the same roadmap as before, still bisexual on the dial, but this is how a grown woman whose husband has been out of town on a business trip would behave if the mailman walked by.

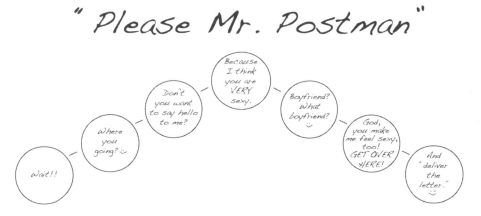

Now that you've seen this interpretation, it kind of makes you wonder if you could do it totally gay, too, if you really heightened the story, right?

Show Them How Your Mind Works

This system is preposterous, I know. It's absurd, unusual, and outrageous. But guess what. It works. My students have been succeeding beyond their wildest dreams using my interpretation of the Kinsey Scale as their creative gauge. I dare you to try it!

The scale is not exact. And nothing else in this book is intended to be taken as black and white rules for do's and don'ts. Everything reported here aims to teach you how to be intuitive with your material, in order that you will be empowered to capture the essence of the show for which you are auditioning.

In the words of Michael Mayer, director of *Spring Awakening*, "Bring intelligence and intuition, and be informed. Create an opportunity to share the way your mind works. In your audition, show us that you are a thinking, aware person who could put yourself in the piece of music. Show us, 'This is how my mind works. This is how my taste is. I can bring interpretation, taste, and understanding.'"[13]

Now go to your DVD and click on "Final Performance" under every genre we've covered in the book to see me put the songs I've used to teach you into action. These final performances incorporate vocal, physical, and interpretive techniques. Note that these "auditions" are specific to where they fall on our version of the Kinsey scale.

What Do I Do with My Body?

H ere is where the intuition you've been developing while reading this book will *really* come in handy. Your soul, your mind, your heart—your everything—is held inside of your body. When you hear the term "mind–body–soul connection," it means this: that everything is connected.

Some people say that if you think negative thoughts, you can make yourself sick. I believe that. I also believe in mind over matter. I believe the body can heal itself. What *you* need to believe for the purpose of performing is that your mind, body, and soul need to be in harmony with each other when you perform. They need to work together in the room.

It is important not to distract people with your body when you're performing, so you have to learn why, when, and how to use it. Your work as a performer is to differentiate between when to use the rhythm you feel in your body and when to stay totally still.

Some songs, like "A Song for You" by Leon Russell and "Let It Be" by Paul McCartney, need stillness. You *can't* allow yourself to show that you feel the rhythm, as it is too damn distracting to those watching you. But standing still *is* a way of using your body. When you are standing still, your body is a vessel. The message you want to convey can only come through clearly in a vessel that is still. If you were to express rhythm in your body, it would shake the vessel, causing your message not to come through clearly.

How to Feel Music in Your Body

Earlier in the book, I spoke of how you are allowed to feel and express rhythm in your body when performing rock music. Now, you need to know that as the music grows, the way you feel the music in your body needs to grow as well. So it's a universally good idea to start out with a relatively still, easy body, and then, as the story unfolds and your emotions build, begin moving more as your connection to the rhythm also grows.

Jen Waldman is an acting teacher with whom I've had a great time studying. I was taking a class with Jen, and she made some remarks about "feeling the music in your body" that are worth sharing. If you understand music in a technical way, this explanation will be perfectly suited for you. Jen says, "Songs were not written for a dramatic purpose. Rather than creating a dramatic arc that is analytical, you create a musically dramatic arc. You need to feel the arc of the music in your body. What we need from you is to see your connection to the intensity, the energy, the progress, and the forward motion of the piece."

She continues, "The arc is found in the pulse of the music. The music creates a chemical reaction that forces you to feel this pulse. Feel the downbeat and sustain that feeling throughout the whole note. As the dramatic arc of the piece comes into play, you will start feeling the half note, then the quarter note, and maybe even the eighth note."[1]

Remember, chickadee, this physical expression doesn't happen with every song. It is not *all* the time. However you need to know that this is a possibility. Later on in the chapter, we're going to dig a little deeper into the subject matter so that it will make more sense to you!

Here's what I want you to know. When people realize they can use their bodies, it's awesome. But feeling the rhythm in your body isn't only tapping your feet. Remember when I told you to rock out with your whole body when you tell the piano player how a song feels? Well, guess what. That's the basis for what we're about to discuss.

How to Use Your Body in an Audition

I have a special treat for you. It's a method I have used successfully for many years. It was influenced and inspired by "viewpoints," a brilliant technique developed by choreographer Mary Overlie in 1970, and adapted for stage acting by Anne Bogart and Tina Landau, two of the greatest theater directors of our time.[2]

Most of the time when we audition, we stand facing forward on the stage with our feet shoulder-length apart and deliver our song. But if rock music insists that we *feel* the rhythm in our body, standing like that is nearly impossible. Therefore, we need an alternative strategy for how to use our body. Here's my suggestion. There's all of this "space around you" that is so valuable and yet rarely explored; it includes the space in front of you, in back of you, along your sides, up above you, and down below you. Explore the space around you to see what *other* options there are for using your body. Exploring this frequently ignored territory is an outstanding way to give an authentic and natural physicality to each and every style of rock musical.

You must only hint at the moves of an era as you sing your audition piece. What you do with your body must be so natural that it appears to be second nature to you. The emotions and the story that you are portraying must be communicated first and foremost above anything else. What you do with your body cannot seem choreographed; rather, it must come out, or be birthed, from how you feel and from how the music moves you. It needs to be the "cherry on top" of the tasty treat that is your performance.

What does this music make you want to do with your body? What does this music feel like in your body? No matter what decade a musical is set in, your acting challenge is to do your best to find an answer. Go back to the DVD, click on "Body," and you'll watch an introduction that will give you a brief description of "the space around you."

The '50s and '60s Body

My student Donell Foreman booked the role of Seaweed in the national tour of *Hairspray,* a show set in 1962. Here is what Donell says led the producers to hire him:

> *Hairspray* is highly stylized. For the auditions, I had to sing a song from the 1960s to show that I have a grasp on the style of the music and that I feel comfortable adjusting my body language to the time period. I chose to sing "(Your Love Keeps Lifting Me) Higher and Higher" by Jackie Wilson. The energy in the '60s was different than it is now. Performers during that period had an insane amount of charisma and stage presence. What needed to come through me was clarity of the details of what this person's love was like, and how love lifted me emotionally "so high" that I couldn't stand still, but had to dance and celebrate how good the love felt in my body. I grabbed the producers' attention by styling my voice to fit the '60s and allowing myself to feel and express the rhythm of the song in my body, while also allowing my own personality and life to shine through.[3]

Feeling the rhythm in their bodies was a big part of the way the performers of the 1960s expressed their feelings. They were so moved that they *had* to move.

Look up '60s artists on YouTube. Study their movements. See how they never let themselves get loose or sloppy. Their emotions were strong, but never out of control. Watch performers like the Spinners, the Four Tops, Jackie Wilson, Aretha Franklin, Diana Ross and the Supremes, and Dusty Springfield. All moved in a measured, polite, simple, and graceful way, and yet there was a tremendous opportunity for them to express their emotions through their bodies.

Popular dances were the Watusi, the Mashed Potato, the Stroll, the Twist, the Pony, and the Slop. I encourage you to learn these dances and then subtly incorporate the way these moves feel in your body into your audition, as they will show up in almost all of the '50s and '60s rock musicals for which you may audition.

Click on "'50s and '60s." Any time you have an audition, simply select the right era to study, and, like magic, instant era!

The '70s Body

Remember our earlier discussion of social changes that occurred during and immediately following the Vietnam War? People went from holding and withholding to literally "letting down their hair." Clothing styles and physical mannerisms swung in the opposite direction of the restraint of the preceding decades. The clothes loosened, the fabrics softened, and people rebelled against a clean-cut way of life. They wanted to get dirty. They didn't want their money to go into the pockets of big business that was profiting off of warfare. If anything was going to change, they felt they had no choice other than to let their feelings out and tell the truth. As a result, the body became free and uninhibited.

People of the decade didn't want to honor the restraints of choreography. When you sing a '70s song, ground yourself. Share an important message that's going to shift the way your audience thinks. Moving your arms and legs in syncopation, as singers did during the '60s, would be a huge distraction from your message.

On your DVD, click on "'70s."

The '80s Body

How should your body be in order to physicalize the 1980s? Both men and women were feminine *and* dramatic. The colors were electric: neon pink, orange, and yellow. Teen idol Debbie Gibson's album was named *Electric Youth* (and so was her perfume). People wore leg warmers, Capezio shoes, and rubber bracelets. Their hair was permed, teased, and crimped with a banana clip in it. Boys and girls both wore mullets. Clothes were usually tight, they wore parachute pants, their shirts had shoulder pads in them. Ties were skinny. Lines were sharp.

With the exception of hard rock, artists of the day were generally gentle on their voices and their bodies, as music became electronically synthesized. To generate the '80s "new wave" body, you have got to think about creating angles. Even people's hair was angular and asymmetrical. The colors were bold, and you must be bold and sharp with your body.

In terms of what you do with your body, watch the videos of the artists who were around in the '80s. They danced in silly ways, but seem to believe absolutely that they were the hottest, sexiest, coolest people around.

This genre of performance is excellent when discussing the physical body because it brings up another important point. Eighties rock invites you to "scream your face off" if you are singing Journey, Foreigner, Def Leppard, or other bands like them. Now, you and I both know that screaming our faces off is no good for our vocal cords. You shouldn't do it. Thus, what you want to do in an audition is work your body in a way that looks like you are exerting yourself—even though you are not. You should only be styling it.

Click on "'80s."

The Contemporary Rock Body

In the 1990s and 2000s, perhaps for the first time, singers began inviting the audience to come see inside of them, inside their soul. They drew people in and began to insist that others see how they felt, as opposed to showing them. The sentiment was intimate, thus the physicality of the body also was. When singing contemporary rock and pop songs, we must be as profoundly still as we are when we sing '70s music. If we were to move, to gesture, it would be distracting and impede letting people into our personal lives. Remember, the body must be a vessel to let the emotion come through.

My student Anthony Lee Medina, who starred as Otto in the national tour of *Spring Awakening,* says:

> When I was in callbacks for *Spring Awakening,* I worked a lot on finding new intentions for the song "Touch Me" from the show. I stood still and simply explored my sexuality. I pictured someone who I deeply desired walking towards me, and imagined what it would be like if they were to touch my face, and run their hand down my neck and over my chest to my stomach, and bend in to kiss me. What emotions was I going through? Fear, excitement, and then wanting. And how did the ache in my voice reflect these emotions? All I did was to feel my feelings and sing them, to style them.[4]

Now, let me emphasize that Anthony didn't "show" the creative team his feelings. He felt his feelings, and thus it made the people behind the table in the audition room think, "I want to understand this misunderstood person." Make sense?

Alex Timbers, director of *Bloody Bloody Andrew Jackson,* says,

> The genesis of the music in *Bloody Bloody Andrew Jackson* is the essence of emo music, a culture-specific subgenre of music that was written for twenty-seven year olds who are singing about the girls who broke their hearts when they were fifteen. That music can be identified as the sound of Weezer, Fall Out Boy, and Dashboard Confessional. Any songs from the album *Jagged Little Pill* by Alanis Morissette and any of Pink's music are also a great example of this essence. In auditions, we really respond to people who bring in contemporary music. It doesn't need to be emo; it just needs to have that attitude. It can be '80s rock. We do an exercise with our auditioners where we make them sing the song with their feet planted wide, chin down, eyes up and focused on a single point, as if they are delivering all their angst and anger through a pinhole."[5]

Click on "Contemporary Rock."

The Contemporary Pop Body

How do you physicalize the last twenty years of the contemporary pop scene? People loved their high-heeled shoes, their furs, their fast cars, and drinking Krystal. Music videos celebrated big pimpin', underaged drinkin', barely-any-clothes-on, definitely-not-wearing-underpants, booty shakin', very sexy, high-energy choreography. The music was hot-hot-hot, sexy, sensual, a little dirty, and seductive. Hip-hop seduction.

Where contemporary rock is dark, contemporary pop music is light, fun, and sexy, so you need to take the space when you are auditioning with a pop song, as if you were a light, fun, sexy artist like Beyoncé, and work it. You do not need to *act* like Beyoncé. You just have to understand *how* she experiences music. If Beyoncé's essence is fierce and empowered, *you* need to be fierce and empowered—in your own way. Offstage, she's reserved. But her public persona is different. For God's sake, she has created an alter ego for her stage work that she calls Sasha Fierce. Quite frankly, she is so fabulous that she is one step *beyond* a drag queen. When she hits the stage, she expresses who she is through her body language and sexuality, and in her strength, dance moves, outrageous energy, and, my god, with her voice! Her soul! *This* is light.

The video you would make for a contemporary pop song is a different kind than for a rock song. This is a sexy video, so you have to draw the audience in or knock them out with your hips. Really, the essence of this way of using the body can be classified as *showmanship*.

Click on "Contemporary Pop."

Now your pop auditions do not have to be as extreme as an A Sasha Fierce production number. Some pop songs don't require that *level* of showmanship. What you must be sure of is that you feel your coolness. Feel your sexiness. Feel the rhythm and let yourself go.

An Onstage Alter Ego

What Beyoncé is doing when she becomes Sasha Fierce is actually what this book is about when you get right down to it. She steps 150 percent into being her alter ego whenever she is performing. For any rock musical audition, like her, you need to create an alter ego that can fool the creative team into thinking this persona, even if it's subtle, has been your nature your whole life. It's smoke and mirrors, but a fabulous show nonetheless!

You in the Audition Room

As rock performers we are not here to fit the mold, we are here to *break* the mold. If you think you haven't shattered the mold into tiny pieces already, there's one more step you can take in breaking yourself free.

Just as your accompanist became your scene partner, now your audition opens up to an even bigger scene in the play. In the words of Michael Mayer:

> The minute you walk in the door you are in a scene with everyone in the room, and you are responsible for how the scene goes. Your song is only one part of the scene. When an actor truly wants to connect—from a real place—to the folks on the other side of the table, it's such a gift. Be present and be a great listener. I want to talk to a human being. When I do, I think, "This is a great scene!" If I have no sense of you as a person, how can I hire you? A cool person usually sounds better on my shows than just a good singer. So does a team player. Life's too short otherwise.[1]

My hope is that if you walk away from reading this book with anything at all, *beyond* understanding how to rock your audition, it would be to have a playful respect for and integrity in your work. So here are a few last ideas I have for you to make *this* scene the best scene in the show I'll call "The Day of Auditions."

1. Before you even get in the audition room, you meet the monitor or casting assistant who is running the audition. Please treat this person with kindness, care, and respect. If you are a sweetheart in the room but a jerk to the monitor, your attitude is going to bite you in the ass later on. I've seen it happen!

2. Find out the accompanist's name, and then greet this individual with clarity, efficiency, and responsibility. Implement everything we

discussed in Chapter 5. If you don't remember what you read, for God's sake go back and look it over!

3. Acknowledge the people behind the table with ease and positivity. Find out who they are before you arrive, and do a bit of research on what they are up to in the world. You may have something in common that you can mention in the room—but only if the energy feels right. Never push for connection. Just be open.

4. Please be intuitive about the distance between you and the table. You need to place yourself at a sufficient distance from the creative team so that they feel like they're in a small theater watching you sing onstage, *not* that they are onstage with you. Intuit the right distance based on the size of the room and where the piano is located.

5. Don't bring your personal problems in the room. This is a job. Be open, yet professional. This particular suggestion is here because I had a very difficult spell of anxiety as a younger performer. I've since learned how to handle my worry, but there remains a casting office or two whose staff knew me during that time, who—even to this day—won't call me in for an audition because my behavior in the audition room was so full of terror. So if you are having a bad day or you're in an insecure place, use your song to confess it and pull you out of it. Start the song from that crappy place you are in, and then use the storyline to help your energy change and grow clearer. This will add another dimension to the work that will make you seem more present and more connected to the listeners. Again . . . and I really mean this . . . save your emotions for the song!

6. Above all else, please, if the show you are planning on auditioning for is currently running on or Off-Broadway, go see it before you audition. There is no excuse for not doing so. Use your student ID, or go online at 8 a.m. and get "rush seats," or purchase a "standing room only" ticket. Most Broadway shows nowadays run a "lottery" two hours before the show starts where people can win discounted tickets. Get a subscription to the Theatre Development Fund (TDF) for discount tickets. At some Off-Broadway theaters, you can even be an usher and watch the show for free.

If you don't actually live in or near the "big city of dreams," or the show is no longer running on Broadway, why leave yourself in the dark? Study your rock musicals in the same way you study legit musical theater. Get your hands on as many soundtracks as you can, and study every rock musical. Why not *live* in an informed way instead of leaving it to the last minute, or worse, showing up to an audition uninformed.

Taking responsibility for your experience is how to be appropriate in the audition room. It is inside of these parameters that you get to break the mold.

Wear Clothing That's Authentic to You

Earlier in the book, we talked a little bit about what to wear for your auditions. My sensibility is that you want to wear clothing that represents who you are as a person, not a costume.

Carrie Gardner and Stephen Kopel from Roundabout Theatre Company/Jim Carnahan Casting

Carrie: I don't care what you wear. Wear what you wear every single day. Ultimately it's not going to get you the job. There is something slightly annoying when people come in full costume, in pigtails, and baby doll dresses. They think they have to wear leather cuffs and chains to be punk. The costume thing? It's not for me. [2]

Stephen: There's also a lack of individuality in the audition outfits we typically see. Guys wear jeans, a vest, a button-up, tie, converse. Girls wear wrap dresses and character shoes. It's like working in a factory. All of these people who look exactly the same coming in and out of the audition room. [3]

Carrie: Every aspect of your audition, including what you wear, tells us something about you. We learn about people's personalities in the way they dress. People don't understand that *your essence* is what's really important. Not your actual outfit. Can we see you in the world of the show? Do you belong? Your outfit doesn't give you that edge . . . who you are does. [4]

You *have* to feel like an authentic human being, because the essence of the show needs to be translated through your being. So wearing something that tries to prove to the casting people that you are a "hippie" or a "punk rocker" only says you think your presence in the music and your innate sense of style aren't enough. Be authentic in everything you do in the audition room.

Since you do want to *hint at* how a person would dress in the show for which you are auditioning, do this with clothing items you already have in your closet. Suggest, don't force—just like you would do in your acting. As Alaine Alldaffer, the casting director at Playwrights Horizons, says, "What you want to do is trick the eye with a touch of the style. But do it only to a point where it's not distracting. What we want to think is 'That person made an effort to include details that give us a hint of his or her potential appearance.' By tricking our eye, it helps us *imagine* what they might look like if we put them inside the picture we are painting in the production, as opposed to them *telling* us." [5]

Basically, if you are able to walk out of the building after your appointment feeling like you are not in a costume, and you can wear that outfit for the rest of the day, you are dressed appropriately.

Nodding to the Piano Player

Nodding to your piano player to start your song is so old school! Remember, accompanists are intuitive. This comes with the territory of being a great musician. So instead of nodding, you can suggest subtler things like, "You can start when I lift my head" or "I'm going to take a deep breath, and then you can start."

If you intend to begin at the piano and move to the center of the room as your intro plays, while you are at the piano say, "Great. You can start." These simple ways of starting the song can take you out of the mode of being someone on an audition and transform you into a human being, which is what everyone wants and needs you to be.

Remember, of course, to say "thank you" after you finish your brilliant performance!

The Focus Spot

Let's talk about the focus spot. In theater, there must always be a focal point for our eyes. This spot has been suggested to be right above the heads of the auditioners in the center of the audition table. Sometimes it's even okay to place this spot at the level of their heads—if you put it *between* their heads. The reason why this focus spot is there in the first place is because once the song starts, the creative team doesn't want to be in the scene with you anymore. They want to be an audience member now. They don't want you to look them in the eyes. So this focus spot represents the person with whom you are now in the scene.

This is all fine and good. But what human being looks at another human being dead-on when they are having a conversation? Think of your own genuine behavior. Don't you ever look away? Don't you ever close your eyes? I know that when I am thinking about something to say to someone, or I am gathering my thoughts, I often take myself away from that person until my thought makes sense. Then when it does, I'm right back with my listener, as if to say, "Do you know what I mean?"

What if you were to *refer* to this person in the focus spot like we refer to each other in real life? When your lyrics are really important, glance over at the person in the focus spot to see if there's a reaction. But don't stand there looking at the focus spot (the "person") the entire time or you'll look like a stalker.

The "X" Mark

In our experience all these years as musical theater performers, have we not entered the room, given the accompanist our music, and hit our mark: the "X" spot on the floor? I mentioned on the DVD exploring the space around you while honoring the "X," remember?

Well guess what? At certain auditions there's even *more* room to play with the space around you. What room do I mean? I mean the audition room.

You see, with a great deal of legit musical theater, and even some rock musicals of the past, the pictures we'd paint in the room were physically still, but we'd paint with huge, broad, loud strokes.

You need to give an intimate and nuanced performance that you'd see on TV now, like *in* a video on MTV or VH1. But it must be so filled with the specificity of your emotions that it can be read and heard all the way to the back row of the theater.

Here are a few ideas of ways to create this "rock video" in an audition.

▶ I mentioned this earlier, but what if you start your song over at the piano and use the introduction to move to the center of the room?

▶ If the room in which you are auditioning is small, what if you start the song leaning against the back wall and then move toward center stage on the dramatic build?

▶ What if you start the song jamming at the piano with the piano player (which could help him grasp the feel) and then move toward the center as the song grows?

▶ If there is a mirror in the audition room, why not pull back the curtain on it and start the song while looking into the mirror?

▶ What if there was a window in the room, on *your* side of the table? Why not start the song looking out the window? Imagine . . . Is the person you are singing about on the way up to your house? How would that make you feel?

Feelings are an essential aspect of your audition. How does it make you feel to look yourself in the eye when you are singing about something painful? How does it make you feel to lean against the wall? Is there an emotional reason to do that? Are you so frail, for instance, that you need the wall to hold you up? Are you worried that you will fall to pieces if you don't lean against it? How does your environment affect your performance?

These are the types of things that make an audition resemble a rock video, and so I wholeheartedly encourage you to try all of the above at least once.

Use the room you are in. Be a human being in a real environment. Break the rules. But before you do . . . here are a few more rules you need to know about breaking the rules!

A Few More Rules

The way you move and use the space in the room *must* apply to the song. You can't do it only for the reason that it is "cool." It has to fit the storytelling. It has to make sense in regard to the style, the sentiment, and the genre. It is appropriate *sometimes,* not all the time.

You need to know when it is important just to stand and sing like a human being, someone who is talking to a friend or your family. This is similar to the idea of the dial on the Kinsey Scale of Acting in Chapter 8. Whether or not to remain in place while you sing depends upon what kind of song you have, and the kind of show for which you are auditioning. Please use your intuition about how much or how little movement to do. If your song is simple, you can trust that it doesn't need any special moves. Just stand there and be in it. That is also a gorgeous picture or rock video you could establish.

Really, you cannot *decide* to do something special like this right before you go into the audition room. You have to treat the song the same way you would a legit musical theater song. You have to rehearse it. You wouldn't learn a Stephen Sondheim piece, an Adam Guettel piece, or a Stephen Schwartz song the *night* before an audition without working out the moments, would you? So you should never learn a rock song last minute without working it out moment by moment. As a rule, never "wing it."

Rock auditioning really *is* the same as auditioning for legit musical theater in many ways. If you are auditioning for Sondheim's *Sunday in the Park with George,* you need to be still, poised, and classic like the painting that the artist Georges Seurat, who is the lead character, paints in the show. On the other hand, if you are auditioning for William Finn, composer of *Falsettos,* you need to feel relaxed and casual, like all of his characters are.

If you are at home, practice your song in front of the mirror. If you are in acting class, and you are in an audition studio or rehearsal room, practice it in the mirror during class. Practice how you will break away from the mirror and move to the center of the room.

If you are at home, practice looking out of your window. Move the chairs out of the way in your living room. Create a stage that has the window as its back wall.

Practice starting the song leaning against your bedroom closet door, and then move to the center of the room when the song grows stronger.

Practice starting your song at different kinds of pianos. Use one that is upright, another that is a baby grand.

Practice standing totally still, without moving a muscle.

Please, I beg you to practice these different approaches to movement.

Get so good at each of them that you can enter a room and, as you are walking in, you will casually notice the size of the room, if there a mirror, if there is a window to look out of, and make a choice of how or when to move.

"But what if there's no mirror," you might ask. "What if the wall is really far back?"

Well, start a little farther back than the intuited "perfect place" you found from which to start your song, and move forward to where the "X" mark is "supposed" to be on the dramatic build of the song. You could also start with your back facing the table and turn around during the introduction. Whatever takes you out of the conventions of legit musical theater auditions is going to look more like a rock video.

Again, I dare you. Will you also do this for your legit auditions? If you are singing "Right as the Rain" by Harold Arlen, will you look out at the window and notice that it's raining, and this is what sparks your idea to sing? Does it spark you to know that a person is right for you like the rain is right for the earth? Once you know this person is right for you, can you move to the center of the room to be with him/her?

You want to paint a picture with your body and then give the impression that the picture changes when your emotions change. Or don't move at all.

Intuit what to do in the audition room. Then you *must* practice that which you decide upon in front of a teacher or supportive friends so that you know the technique you've settled on is appropriate for the song you are singing.

I bet you are like, "Oh my God, Sheri! Enough with telling me to practice!" Here's why I am so insistent on it.

The work that goes on in my class is magical. The breakthroughs are kind of profound. My students walk out feeling like they are on fire. Then, maybe like a month later, they'll have an audition that will require the rock song we worked on. And they will go in assuming they'll nail it like the learned to do in my classroom, and they bomb. Because between their nerves and never practicing it, the work they do doesn't carry. If they practiced, even once a day (that's a one-minute song sung once a day), that song would have found its way into their cells, into their bloodstream. It would have become so real and true to them. You are a better performer when you are ready. You must be ready for them to say yes to you.

Your Hands

Let's talk about the subject of your hands. Remember? Hands are for eating and wiping your butt. If you want to use them in your rock audition, use them in a way that serves the story and the feeling of the music in your body. You really don't need your hands to help me understand how you feel. But you need to show me how you feel by showing me how the music makes you feel in your body, and your hands can be a part of this demonstration.

Closing Your Eyes

You aren't allowed to close your eyes at all in legit musical theater auditions. But when you watch rock singers onstage, their eyes are closed most of the time because they're feeling the music and evoking a sound. In a rock musical audition, you are therefore allowed to close your eyes. But only once, in a meaningful place.

Just as you should not overuse your hands, don't close your eyes so much that you take yourself away from us.

Get into the Emotional Zone

How do I tap into some of the more painful emotions when I have to be positive and nice and sweet and kind in the audition room?

Here is Michael McElroy, back again with a great anecdote. Did you see him in *Violet,* Deaf West Theatre's production of *Big River, Rent,* or the original Broadway production of *Tommy*? If you did, then you can believe he's *really* good at this.

> Prepare to get into the zone. Way before the audition. Say you have a boyfriend, who didn't bring the garbage out for the twentieth time and you wait for him to come home. And you are *upset.* He finally comes home, but he comes home with his mother. So now you have to be nice. It's not that you're not upset, but you do meet and greet her politely and kindly. Then you let him have it when she's gone. It's like that with auditioning. Get in the zone, come in and do the meet and greet, start letting it come back in the minute you head for that piano player (still polite and kind, of course).
>
> The minute you walk away from that piano you are living it, living in that moment. Once the music starts you're there emotionally where you need to be. This begins before you open your mouth to sing. Fearlessness is based on knowledge, understanding, and history. Once you have all that, then you can come in the room, and just *live.*[6]

Life, Career, and Limitations

Here is wisdom from more of the greats of musical theater, a few you've met, others to whom I am introducing you now. Let's begin with casting director Stephanie Klapper. She has cast numerous Broadway and Off-Broadway musicals, among others, *Bells Are Ringing, Dividing the Estate, an oak tree,* additional casting for *It Ain't Nothin' but the Blues, Venice* (co-casting with Bonnie Grisan), *In Transit* (with Primary Stages), and Moises Kaufman's *Into the Woods.* She's taken good care of me over the years in my career as an actor. I also love what she has to say about auditions:

> Don't expect perfection. Throw caution to the wind, have a blast, and do the best you can while honoring all of the artists involved in the production by doing the research and being prepared. What we are looking for in this medium is not having a censor. That's what's different about rock musicals and legit musicals. In rock, you are allowed to be much more human, flawed, and imperfect if you connect to your material in a visceral, truthful way. You can be messy. You have permission to be. An audition for *Light in the Piazza* has to be pristine and delicate. It's a fine painting. It's not a Jackson Pollock or a Keith Haring painting. Those would be rock auditions. As long as what you show us is who you really are, it's fine to be it. You are saying, "I am allowing myself to be imperfect in front of you [the creative team] because I am being authentic with you."[7]

Wise casting woman and friend Cindi Rush has this to say:

> Actors get beaten up because they take "rejection" too personally. What screws actors up the most—a point they need to understand—is that intrinsically musical theater is a buy-and-sell marketplace. That which they are selling is themselves. It's a business. The nature of our business is that you must know yourself so well that you are not influenced by everything outside of you, but instead present enough within yourself and what you do well to say, "This is who I am" and "This is what I give," "This is what I do well" and "This is what I have to work on," and it is very little to do with how the casting people respond.
>
> You just have to show up. That's life. You have to show up anywhere, you have to find a way to say, "This is who I am," and if who you are is not who the casting people want for their project, it's fine because it has nothing to do with you. Leave it to them to decide. There is nothing you can do to force them to see you as you want to be seen. Come in being who you are and they will decide."[8]

Scott Wojcik and Gayle Seay from Wojcik-Seay Casting shared the following pearls of integrity-filled advice. Scott began:

> Everyone has a light inside them; I think an actor's light shines brighter. Performers are special creatures. They burn brighter, and it is that intensity that draws an audience in, or it gets turned internally and destroys and ruins their heart and their soul. This business ruins people. Sometimes in an audition, the actor walks out of the room before they walk in. The desperation is palpable and the people behind the table can feel that. Some auditioners are always trying to "crack the code" or trying to second guess what it is those behind the table are looking for, trying to get "one up" on us. You can't. One approach is to remember the joy in performing. You have to. That's the key. Singing from a place of joy assists in communicating the honesty of the idea of the lyric. It has to come from that place. Have a sense of self-value. Can you treat this like it is fun and you love playing with people? Because at the end of the day, an audition is a job interview. It's a job, it isn't your life.[9]

Gayle continues: "Your performance is an example of the casting director's taste and point of view. Think about the situation that the casting people are in. We are all under pressure to solve this puzzle. Let's work together to do this. We, as casting directors, are your advocates. We care about your success. Plus, if you solve our puzzle we look awesome! So, you have to take that leap. Be fearless. I promise, we will catch you."[10]

Lady Alaine at Playwrights Horizons asserts:

> Respecting the craft is not just about you getting the part. It's about asking, "What can I contribute to this process? Who can I be to contribute to the vision of this piece?" Actors have a fear of being vulnerable. Vulnerability is a beautiful gift you give yourself. If you are vulnerable, you've contributed. Every person who comes in teaches us about what we are casting. We learn from people's interpretations. When you bring your creativity into the room, you are contributing even if you haven't gotten the part. There's a lot that is not fair about this business. You can't crack the code. It's not logical. And because it's not logical, there's freedom in it; you can do whatever you want. Your energy could be expended where you can be bettering yourself in every way. Art can change and heal the world. Go in and do your part and heal people. Be a mirror for the audience so that we can see what needs changing and what needs healing in our lives.

When you are waiting to audition, it helps to bless the people you meet in the hallway. Bless the people in the room. Something happens on a molecular level when we bless another person. Counting one's blessings strengthens the immune system.

Don't give your power away. I liken an audition to the story of *The Wizard of Oz,* and you're filling in for Dorothy. You go to see the great and powerful wizard (the casting director, the creative team), who seems to have the power to make or break you. But he doesn't really. It is tempting to give the casting team too much power. Remember, *you are wearing the ruby slippers.*[11]

Be the kind of actor who brings us back to where we came from, back home to ourselves by showing us qualities like integrity, care, respect, responsibility, passion, commitment, generosity, creativity, and fun.

If you've been on line outside the audition room for a while and have heard other actors screaming rock songs, even if you were originally planning to sing a song like that, take a moment, switch gears, and sing something intimate and private. Be sensitive. Change the energy in the room! Be the person who lets the creative team breathe.

Know Thyself, Including Thy Limitations

In this great soul search you are doing in order to make a contribution to musical theater, there is a significant element that I do not want to leave out. It's okay to have limitations. Not only is it okay to have limitations; it's very cool, conscious, and professional of you to know your own limitations. You will absolutely grow and become a more dynamic and brilliant performer by listening to all sorts of music and learning all sorts of styles. Please understand, however, that while you may be great at Motown or awesome at '90s pop, you shouldn't get dressed up like a punk and go in for *American Idiot* if this genre is not a part of you ready to be cultivated and brought out.

If a style is not in your nature, don't try to force it. The folks behind the table know when a role is not a natural fit for an actor. Again, a leather cuff and a spiky hairdo won't make you a punk rocker. Punk has to be inside of you. If it's not inside of you, that is okay. There are plenty of other things that are inside of you to be brought out onstage.

Finally, advice from Geoff Johnson, formerly of Johnson/Liff Casting, a man I consider theater royalty. Along with his business partner, the beloved Vinny Liff, Geoff won the only Tony Award ever presented to a casting office in the history of Broadway musical theater. True gentlemen of the theater community, these guys set the bar of professionalism and care higher than heaven. Geoff says: "Casting directors just love to claim, 'Oh, I gave this person their big break, I gave that person their big break.' In truth, they don't give any actor their big break. An actor does. Actors give themselves their big breaks. We merely hold the door open for them to come through. Give yourself the big break that you deserve."[12]

Ten years from now, all the rock musicals will be different. The shows that are on Broadway today may be revived, and who knows? Maybe Jay-Z and Beyoncé will write a hip-hop musical together. What will remain the same, however, is the necessity for you as a performer to study the essence of music, and share your connection to it with care, detail, joy, generosity, and vulnerability. We need you. Don't ever forget that.

Final Thoughts for the Actor

O h my God. I just wrote a book.

I'm a musical theater performer and teacher. But I proposed a book idea, wrote a book proposal, got a book deal, and in seven months I wrote a book all by myself. I was entirely responsible for every aspect of this book being written. I interviewed everyone in this book, researched the rock music and rock music history, applied and negotiated the rights to use these songs as teaching tools, shot the DVD, helped edit my own book, *and* worked fulltime as a teacher. I even worked four times as an actress during this insanity.

Imagine what you would be like as a performer if you committed to your craft in the same way I committed to doing this book.

I asked for help. I had a roundtable where my acting teacher, a friend who is a voice teacher, and four students read two chapters a week with me so that I could see if my language translates, since normally I show people how to act rather than tell them.

I was not a writer. There were times when I didn't know how to say the things that I am so good at showing people how to do. So I borrowed money, and I hired a writing coach to help me put language to my feelings in those spots.

If I could do this, you could be a rock musical theater performer. From this day forward, don't you dare say, "I'm not a rock singer." Yes, you are.

And I am a writer.

Ask for help.

This book isn't perfect. I made mistakes. There are things I wish I had time to fix. But I did it. It's my history, my terror, and my healing, all channeled into my creativity. And it's messy and flawed. But it's real. And it's who I am. And I am sharing it with you. As is. And it feels really good.

Earlier in my career, the theater community handed me superstardom, and I said no to it. I sabotaged it. I was scared of succeeding.

This book is me saying yes—yes to everything that is possible for me.

Yes to everything I once said no to.

Say yes.

Notes

Chapter 1

1. Rob Meffe is former associate conductor of the Broadway company of *Les Miserables*. Email correspondence, October 2010.
2. Ibid.
3. Burt Bacharach. Personal interview, October 7, 2010.
4. Elizabeth L. Wollman. *The Theater Will Rock* (Ann Arbor: University of Michigan Press, 2006): p. 40.
5. Ibid: p. 118.
6. Andrew Zerman. Personal interview, October 5, 2010.
7. Stephen Oremus. Personal interview, October 11, 2010.
8. Bernie Telsey. Personal interview, October 19, 2010.
9. Ibid.
10. David Clemmons. Personal interview, September 20, 2010.
11. Telsey.
12. Carrie Gardner and Stephen Kopel. Personal interview, September 9, 2010.
13. Telsey.

Chapter 2

1. Jay Binder. Personal interview, February 10, 2010.
2. Andy Blankenbuehler. Personal interview, September 19, 2010.
3. "Discover Elvis," Elvis.com.

Chapter 3

1. Source: Memphisthemusical.com.
2. William Kloman, "Laura Nyro: She's the Hippest—and Maybe the Hottest," *New York Times* (October 6, 1968), as cited by Michele Kort in *Soul Picnic: The Music and Passion of Laura Nyro* (New York: Thomas Dunne Books, 2002): p. 60.
3. Source: allbusiness.com/humanities-social-science/visual-performing-arts-music/13322257-1.html.
4. Dave Clemmons. Personal interview, September 20, 2010.
5. Cindi Rush. Personal interview, July 29, 2010.

6. Ibid.
7. Michael McElroy. Personal interview, September 21, 2010.
8. Carmel Dean. Personal interview, September 16, 2010.
9. VP Boyle. Personal interview, September 14, 2010.

Chapter 4

1. Cindi Rush. Personal interview, July 29, 2010.
2. Dave Clemmons. Personal interview, September 20, 2010.

Chapter 5

1. Adam Wachter. Personal interview, August 25, 2010.
2. Ibid.
3. Eddie Rabin. Personal interview, September 29, 2010.
4. Ibid.
5. Ibid.
6. Wachter.
7. Rabin.
8. Wachter.
9. Ibid.
10. Eddie Rabin. Email correspondence, October 27, 2010.
11. Wachter.

Chapter 6

1. Terry Bloomfield.
2. Tom Kitt. Personal interview, September 22, 2010.
3. Ibid.
4. Alex Lacamoire. Personal interview, August 24, 2010.
5. Stephen Oremus. Personal interview, October 11, 2010.
6. Michael McElroy. Personal interview, September 21, 2010.
7. Lacamoire.

Chapter 7

1. *Rudolph, the Red-nosed Reindeer*. Written by Robert May and Romeo Muller. First aired December 6, 1964. Source: Imdb.com.

2. Linda Winer. "She's Gonna Make It After All/Sutton Foster Breaks out in Inspired 'Millie,'" *Newsday* (April 19, 2002).

3. Gayle Seay from Wojcik-Seay Casting. Personal interview, July 29, 2010.

4. Paula Murray Cole. Personal interview, September 1, 2010.

5. Source: Indiacurry.com.

6. From the Rasaboxes.com website: "Rasaboxes offers performers a concrete physical tool to access, express, and manage their feelings/ emotions within the context of performance.Basically, rasaboxes trains participants to physically express eight key emotions first identified in the Natyasastra, a Sanskrit text dealing with theatre, dance, and music. Rasaboxes integrates this ancient theory with contemporary emotion research about the 'brain in the belly' (the enteric nervous system), studies in facial expression of emotion, neuroscience, and performance theory—including Antonin Artaud's provocative assertion that the actor is 'an athlete of the emotions.'"

The *Natya Sastra* is the oldest surviving text on stagecraft in the world. It is believed to have been written by Bharata Muni between 200 A.D. and 200 B.C. (Source: Chandrakantha. com).

7. Michael Mayer. Personal interview, September 25, 2010.

Chapter 8

1. Source: En.wikipedia.org/wiki/Alfred_ Kinsey.

2. Source: Kinseyinstitute.org/research/ ak-hhscale.html.

3. Cindi Rush. Personal interview, July 29, 2010.

4. Paula Murray Cole. Personal interview, September, 2010.

5. Michael Mc Elroy.Personal interview, September 1, 2010.

6. Alaine Alldaffer. Personal interview, September 1, 2010.

7. Larry O'Keefe. Personal interview, September 22, 2010.

8. Kerry Butler. Personal interview, October 14, 2010.

9. Ibid.

10. O'Keefe.

11. Michael Minarik. Email interview, December 2009.

12. Alex Timbers. Personal interview, August 26, 2010.

13. Michael Mayer. Personal interview, September 25, 2010

Chapter 9

1. Jen Waldman. Personal interview, September 12, 2010.

2. Anne Bogart and Tina Landau. *The Viewpoints Book: A Practical Guide to Viewpoints and Composition* (New York: Theatre Communications Group, 2005).

3. Donnell Foreman. Email correspondence, December 2009.

4. Anthony Lee Medina. Email correspondence, December 2009.

5. Alex Timbers. Personal interview, August 26, 2010.

Chapter 10

1. Michael Mayer. Personal interview, September 25, 2010.

2. Carrie Gardner. Personal interview, September 9, 2010.

3. Stephen Kopel. Personal interview, September 9, 2010.

4. Gardner.

5. Alaine Alldaffer. Personal interview, September 1, 2010.

6. Michael McElroy. Personal interview, September 25, 2010.

7. Stephanie Klapper. Personal interview, September 28, 2010.

8. Cindi Rush. Personal interview, July 29, 2010.

9. Scott Wojcik. Personal Interview, July 29, 2010.

10. Gayle Seay. Personal interview, July 29, 2010.

11. Alaine Alldaffer. Personal interview, September 1, 2010.

12. Rachel Hoffman and Justin Huff. Roundtable discussion, September 16, 2010.

13. Geoff Johnson. Personal interview, October 13, 2010.

Resources

Now that you've learned how to rock your auditions, if you want to further your "rock-abilities," I've created additional resources and programs just for you. These include master and advanced master classes, along with one-day, three-day, and five-day college and summer program workshops. I also offer Repertoire coaching in person or by Skype and iChat, and career coaching for actors, teachers, and young business owners.

Rock the Audition
rock-the-audition.com

Recommended Books

A New Earth: Awakening to Your Life's Purpose by Eckhart Tolle (New York: Penguin 2008).

The Viewpoints Book: A Practical Guide to Viewpoints and Composition by Anne Bogart and Tina Landau (New York: Theatre Communications Group 2005).

Actor Training the Laban Way: An Integrated Approach to Voice, Speech, and Movement by Barbara Adrian (New York: Allworth Press 2008).

Sanford Meisner on Acting by Sanford Meisner (New York: Vintage 1987).

True and False: Heresy and Common Sense for the Actor by David Mamet (New York: Vintage 1999).

Girls Like Us: Carole King, Joni Mitchell, Carly Simon—and the Journey of a Generation by Sheila Weller (New York: Washington Square Press 2009).

She's a Rebel: The History of Women in Rock & Roll by Gillian G. Garr (Berkeley, CA: Seal Press 2002).

Fever: How Rock 'n' Roll Transformed Gender in America by Tim Riley (New York: Picador 2005).

Who Shot Rock and Roll: A Photographic History, 1955–Present by Gail Buckland (New York: Knopf 2009).

The Rock Musician: 15 Years of Interviews—The Best of Musician Magazine by Tony Scherman (New York: St. Martin's Griffin 1994).

The Theater Will Rock: A History of the Rock Musical from "Hair" to "Hedwig" by Elizabeth L. Wollman (Ann Arbor: University of Michigan Press 2009).

Websites
TED: Ideas Worth Spreading
Ted.com

Tom Burke
Tomburkevoice.com

Rasaboxes
Rasaboxes.org

Actors' Equity
Actorsequity.org

Backstage
Backstage.com

Playbill
Playbill.com

Broadway World
Broadwayworld.com

Billboard
Billboard.com

Rolling Stone
Rollingstone.com

Pandora Radio
Pandora.com

Index

About the Author

Sheri Sanders is an actor, singer, and rock audition coach. She teaches Rock the Audition, a master class in auditioning for rock musicals, Advanced Rock the Audition, and is a rock music repertoire and music styling coach. She has taught at Pace University, Syracuse University (the Tepper Semester), Millikin University, and the conservatory at the Papermill Playhouse, Hartt School of Music, Jersey City University, and Westminster Choir College. She has also taught Rock the Audition at Perry-Mansfield Performing Arts School & Camp, TVI Actors Studio, the Network, Actors Connection, Capes Coaching, Making It on Broadway, and Paul Green's School of Rock.

As a performer, Sanders's rock musical credits include the roles of the "Black Boys" Soloist and Mother in *Hair* (with Encores! at City Center); she covered all three band members of Betty in *Betty Rules* (the Zipper); Georgie Bukatinsky in three different productions of *The Full Monty;* and the Senator in *Caligula* (New World Stages). At the Eugene O'Neill Theatre Center, under the direction of Michael Bush, she originated Amy in Paul Scott Goodman's *Easterhouse,* Eve in Michael Aman's *Secrets of Songwriting* (music and some lyrics by Randi Michaels), and had the honor of being in *Stone Soul Picnic: A Tribute to Laura Nyro*. She played Serena Katz in the National Tour of *Fame* and the Hippie in Lowdermilk-Kerrigan's *The Woman Upstairs* at the New York Musical Theatre Festival.

Sanders's legit musical theater credits include the role of Kitty in *The Screams of Kitty Genovese* (New York Musical Theatre Festival), her comic turn as Little Becky in the National Tour of *Urinetown,* Mme. Squirrel in *Emmet Otter's Jugband Christmas* at the Goodspeed Opera House, the Kolokolo Bird in *Just So* at the Goodspeed Opera House, and Susan in *Tom Jones* at the North Shore Musical Theatre.

Sanders holds group classes and private one-on-one coaching sessions in Manhattan. In February 2010, *Backstage,* the most treasured theatrical newspaper in New York City, published an article on Rock the Audition, detailing Sanders's work in the demystification of the rock musical. This was the first article ever written on the subject. From that article, Sanders was chosen for the pilot episode of *My Time,* for the Oprah Winfrey Network.

She resides in Brooklyn, New York.